I0119235

Dept. of Engineering, California, James Ayers

The Sewage Question in California

report of the state engineer, Wm. Ham. Hall, to the Board of Directors of

the Stockton Insane Asylum on the sewerage for the institution in their

charge

.

Dept. of Engineering, California, James Ayers

The Sewage Question in California
*report of the state engineer, Wm. Ham. Hall, to the Board of Directors of the
Stockton Insane Asylum on the sewerage for the institution in their charge*

ISBN/EAN: 9783337367459

Printed in Europe, USA, Canada, Australia, Japan

Cover: Foto ©Andreas Hilbeck / pixelio.de

More available books at **www.hansebooks.com**

STATE

BOARD OF D...

SEWERAG...

SACRAMENTO:

STATE OFFICE, ... JAMES J. AYERS, SUPT. STATE PRINTING.

1883.

OFFICE OF THE STATE ENGINEER, CALIFORNIA, }
SACRAMENTO, August 30, 1883. }

The Honorable Board of Directors of the Stockton Insane Asylum:

GENTLEMEN: The question of sewerage for your institution naturally divides itself into two parts:

The *First*—What shall be done with the sewage matter?

The *Second*—By means of what works and appliances shall it be disposed of?

The ultimate determination of each of these questions involves a consideration of the other, but the study must commence with the first mentioned.

This report is divided into five parts; the first four being devoted to the *first* question above mentioned, and the last one to the *second* question, as follows:

Part 1—The Pollution of Rivers and Estuaries.
Part 2—The Application of Sewage to Land.
Part 3—The Artificial Treatment of Sewage.
Part 4—The Disposal of the Asylum Sewage.
Part 5—The Sewage Works Proposed at the Asylum.

In submitting this paper I do not apologise for requiring so much of your time as it will take to read a long report, because I am impressed with the magnitude of the subject, and with a sense of the fact that we are about to take a step which will be looked to as having been a precedent, when in the future this sewage disposal question shall have attracted as much attention here as it has in older countries; and I feel that it is our duty as officers of the State to leave behind a record of the fact that we have looked deeper than the surface of the matter, and tried, at least, to start aright.

Very respectfully,
Your obedient servant,

WM. HAM. HALL,
State Engineer.

WHAT IS TO BE DONE WITH SEWAGE?

PART 1—THE POLLUTION OF RIVERS AND ESTUARIES.

THE EFFICIENCY OF SEWERAGE WORK.

Every sewerage proposition must be considered from the standpoint of efficiency as well as from that of cost.

To be *efficient* such a system must effect the final disposition of the sewage matter in a way unobjectionable alike to the locality sewered, to other localities, and the public generally.

The question of efficiency in sewerage systems has received very much attention within the past few years.

European centers of population, and outlying districts as well, have been thoroughly shaken in their social structures by this sewage question, and are yet earnestly considering it.

And even in the comparatively young communities of our Eastern States such sanitary matters occupy a prominent place in the minds of the thinking people of all leading cities and suburban neighborhoods, and have received fitting recognition at the hands of professional and scientific men.

As the result of this activity of practice, observation, and thought, there is a fund of experience for us to contemplate.

The professional man who undertakes to look beyond the surface of this subject finds at his command a library of recorded experiences and facts, which are multiplying so rapidly that there is no branch of applied science at this time more progressive than that known as Sanitary Engineering.

No questions in this connection have received more earnest attention than those of the efficiency of the disposal of sewage;

first, by mingling it with the waters of streams and tidal estuaries; and *second*, by applying it to land; and, as auxiliary to each or both of these, *third*, the question of the artificial treatment of sewage matter to render it more easy of efficient final disposal by the other mentioned methods.

The sewage to be dealt with at your institution is simply fouled water—that is, it is "water carried," and not "middenstead" matter.

The object of all sewerage work in dealing with this class of sewage must be to return the water to its natural state of purity, and to change to harmless, if not useful, forms, the other constituent parts of the substance treated.

THE POLLUTION OF WATERS.

The practice of the disposal of sewage by mingling it with the waters of rivers, tidal estuaries, etc., has been upheld upon the theory that running waters soon purify themselves: that the organic matters become changed in character, and other objectionable parts so far dispersed or altered as to lose appreciable influence upon the human senses and all harmful effect upon the human system.

It was alleged that the particles of the organic (animal and vegetable) parts of noxious matters, being dispersed by mingling with comparatively large bodies of water when dumped into a river or estuary, were brought in contact with the combined or dissolved oxygen of the air in the water, or of the air over the water, by the rolling or boiling motion of the current, and thus oxidized—a change equivalent in its effect to *burning*.

The theory appeared to be well founded. A number of instances were cited where the waters of streams polluted by sewage, apparently cleared themselves by running a few miles. Others were brought forward where clear water streams polluted by peaty matter, and rendered dark and opaque by the vegetable organic matter held in solution, became clear after running similarly short distances. These changes it was said were due to oxidation of the animal matter in the one case, and the vegetable matter in the other; and, hence, that the waters were purified.

And it was argued that contact with air under these conditions of mingling with water, having this effect of oxidizing organic matter in these cases, it would have such effect in all cases, and, hence, the mingling of sewage with running or tide agitated waters was not a vicious and objectionable practice.

So well grounded has this theory appeared, and so strong were the interests involved in its favor, that in England, "until "recently, sanitary engineers have done their best to remove "sewage matter from towns into rivers in obedience to legisla-"tive requirements." (Bailey Denton, Lectures, etc., p. 248.)

But for years there has been the most violent opposition to this "pernicious and disgusting practice," throughout Western Europe, but more especially in England, where the subject has been forced to the front in ways that could not be ignored, and where the form of laws and social organization appears to have allowed wider range to the discussion than it attained in the other countries.

But facts soon proved that the theory of self-purification of river waters was at fault. Some streams of no less but greater volume, receiving no more or perhaps less sewage, did not purify their waters as was alleged of others, and inquiry developed the fact that by no means all peaty waters become pure in their onward flow.

And, most perplexing of all, it was observed that streams which for years had received sewage matter without much apparent detriment to their waters, became foul to every sense, within a comparatively short space of time, and without any considerable increase in the amount of sewage led into them.

The subject now assumed a serious form. Great sewerage works had been carried out, immense manufactories located and operated, and all depending for efficiency upon the privilege of a free outfall for sewage into the tidal or inland waterways of the country.

The battle now became fierce. Sanitarians generally, and towns located low down on the streams, protested against the pollution of the waters by town sewage and manufacturing offal at points above.

The property owners ("rate payers," so called in English literature—really non-resident landlords in many instances) in towns where sewerage works had been constructed leading the sewage into the streams, as well as those in other towns which desired to construct works on this principle, together with the manufacturers generally, who were for getting rid of their offal waters in the easiest way to avoid further expense to themselves, vigorously opposed interference with existing practices.

The fight now became a war very similar to the struggle which has gone on in this State between the hydraulic miners and the farmers and others in the Sacramento Valley, with not so much organization of the contending parties, however; but with legal points on both sides, and denial and assertion of facts in a way almost identical.

The objection urged that the waters were rendered unfit for drinking purposes was answered by saying that they ought to be filtered, and that all waters ought to be filtered before drinking, anyhow. About this stage of the contention other towns and cities resorted to filtering their water supplies, and supplying companies were forced by legislative enactment to maintain filter beds in connection with their works.

In the meantime the attention of scientific men had been secured, and a store of systematically arranged facts was accumulating from observation and experiment. The aid of chemistry had been invoked and waters were subjected to chemical analysis with comparatively satisfactory but sometimes startling results, for waters which had been regarded as pure and which were so to all appearance, taste, and smell, were shown to be laden with organic matter of a character calculated to develop the most deadly zymotic diseases under conditions favorable for such development.

Some apparent cases of self-purification of streams were shown to be delusive : the waters were *clarified* and *deodorized* but not *purified* either of their organic impurities or inorganic elements not to be desired in potable waters.

The next step towards the truth was the result of systematic studies into the causes of apparent self-purification of river waters in some instances, by which results the old theory of the oxidation of organic matters by contact with the air, and the consequent purification of river waters, as heretofore stated, is shown to have been altogether in error.

It is now known that, *as a general thing*, waters polluted by the organic matter of sewage do not purify themselves within any limited space of time or distance of flow, as has been supposed, and in no material degree by the sole action of the oxygen contained in the water or of the air above it.

It is certain that alleged cases of self-purification are only apparent to the eye and sense of smell, and are not real ; and it is contended that if waters are dangerous to health they had better have the noxious appearance and smell, and thus carry with them a warning of their character, than be tempting to the eye or lulling in effect.

It is explained that the action of self-purification of rivers of organic matter, found to take place in some cases, is due to the admixture from tributary streams or springs along their banks, of other waters having certain mineral substances (such as ferric oxide, copper, and allumina) in solution, or to the action of certain clays or the mineral constituents of certain clays which compose their bed or banks ; and hence that such instances of self-purification are due to peculiar circumstances, which, being local and not generally distributed, establish the rule as against self-purification at all.

It is understood that the action of the soil of the banks or bed of a stream in purifying its waters of organic matter, after awhile ceases, and that in the mean time the soil itself has become foul and poisoned to a degree that its effect upon the water, were it really purified above, would be to re-impart a noxious organic matter to it in a considerable degree.

SOME AUTHORITIES ON THE SUBJECT.

The line of authorities in support of these general conclusions is so very extended that any attempt to give a fair idea of them in a hurriedly prepared paper as this one must be, would be futile ; and at the same time it should be remarked that opinions are not all one way. A careful tracing of the subject, however, has led me to the conclusions which I have given ; and I believe that any one at all competent to judge of scientific argument, acquainted with the standing of the leading men who have appeared in it, and who will laboriously trace the subject through the records of the original authorities, will find them overwhelmingly in support of the propositions I have laid down, both as to bearing of facts and argument.

A few citations will show their general tone on this point of the pollution of river waters :

The Rivers Pollution Commission.

Consequent upon the rapid deterioration in the quality of river waters in England, and upon the growing opposition to the mingling of sewage with them, in 1865, by authority of law, a Royal Commission was appointed to inquire into the subject.

Men of the very highest professional and scientific standing and widest experience were appointed to the Board. Sir Robert Rawlinson, Past President of the Institution of Civil Engineers ; John T. Harrison, Esq., Member of the Institution, and of the Local Government Board of the Kingdom, and Professor John T. Way, one of the leading chemists of the country, being the members.

In the first report of this Board (pp. 18 to 22) is to be found a summary of the extended series of experiments upon the subject of "self-purification of river waters," and it is conclusively shown that the idea is a fallacy—that purification in any considerable degree, except in very rare cases, does not take place.   This report raised a perfect storm of opposition supposed to be in the interest of capital interested in property and works that would have to be heavily taxed if any change was made in the manner of disposing of sewage.

In 1868 the Queen commissioned a new set of members of the Rivers Pollution Commission.   These were Sir W. T. Denison, Colonel in the Corps of Royal Engineers; Edward Frankland, Esq., one of the most eminent chemists of the present age; and John C. Morton, Esq., an eminent sanitarian.

This was a collection of eminent men charged, by the terms of their commission, with the duty of "inquiring how far the present use of rivers or running waters in England for the purpose of carrying off the sewage of towns and populous places, and the refuse arising from industrial processes and manufactures, can be prevented without risk to the public health or serious injury to such processes and manufactures, and how far such sewage and refuse can be utilized and got rid of otherwise than by discharge into rivers or running waters, or rendered harmless before reaching them," etc.

For the sake of brevity, I quote only from the sixth report of the Commission, issued in 1874, it being the latest to hand at this day.

Under the head of *"Quality of water from different sources,"* the Commission say:

"6. *River water*, usually in England, but less generally in Scotland,
"consists chiefly of the drainage from land which is more or less culti-
"vated.   When it is further polluted by the drainage of towns and
"inhabited places, or by the foul discharges from manufactories, its
"use for drinking and cooking becomes fraught with great risk to
"health.   A very large proportion of the running waters of Great
"Britain are either at present thus dangerous or are rapidly becoming
"so."   (Sixth Rept. Riv. Poll. Com., p. 425.)

Under the heading, *"As to the possibility of rendering polluted water again wholesome:"*

"1. When the sewage of towns or other polluting organic matter "is discharged into running water the suspended matters may be more "or less perfectly removed by subsidence and filtration, but the foul "organic matters in solution are very persistent. They oxidize very "slowly, and they are removed only to a slight extent by sand filtra- "tion. There is no river in the United Kingdom long enough to "secure the oxidation and destruction of any sewage which may be "discharged into it, even at its source." (Work cited, p. 427.)

And, finally, for the purpose of this special point in my subject, I quote a paragraph found under the heading—"*As to the Propagation of Epidemic Diseases by Potable Water :*"

" 1. The existence of specific poisons capable of producing cholera " and typhoid fever is attested by evidence so abundant and strong " as to be practically irresistible. These poisons are contained in the " discharges from the bowels of persons suffering from these diseases."

" 2. The admixture of even a small quantity of these infected dis- " charges with a large volume of drinking water is sufficient for the " propagation of those diseases amongst persons using such water."

" 3. The most efficient artificial filtration leaves in water much " invisible matter *in suspension*, but constitutes no effective safeguard " against the propagation of these epidemics by polluted water. " Boiling the infected water for half an hour is a probable means of " destroying its power of communicating these diseases." (Work cited, p. 427.)

The Metropolitan Water Supply Commission.

Another systematic examination of a portion of this subject was conducted by a Royal Commission similarly authorized by law, known as the "*Water Supply Commission.*"

It was charged with an inquiry into resources of the country to meet the rapidly increasing demand for pure water for the use of the great metropolitan towns and cities of the kingdom.

Composed of the (afterwards) President of Her Majesty's Privy Council (the Duke of Richmond); the President of the Institu- tion of Civil Engineers (Mr. T. E. Harrison); the late President of the Geological Society and Professor of Geology at Oxford (Mr. J. Prestwich); and the Chairman of the Metropolitan Board of Works (Sir J. Thwaites), this Commission also ranks high as a scientific and practical authority. It had ample means at its disposal to employ the men best suited to conduct the work of the investigation, and we must accept its conclusions, which were that the great cities might continue to derive water from the rivers; *provided*, that there was supplied "perfect filtration and efficient measures for excluding the sewage and other pollutions." (Bailey Denton, Lectures; p. 44.)

Experimental Work.

Scientifically and practically. this subject has been quite thoroughly investigated by the first experimentalists of England and France. Here is a brief outline of points made in one line of discussion immediately connected with it:

M. Pasteur.

M. Pasteur, a French chemist, whose professional standing is so high that his researches are frequently spoken of as being classical, has shown that even at a temperature of 30° C. "the oxygen of the air has but a trifling action on extremely "changeable material, such as the albuminoid matter in yeast "water, or a solution of sugar." (*"Annales de Chimie et de Physique," 3d series, vol. LXIV, pp. 35 and 36, also p. 71.*)

This fact, of course, goes contrary to the old theory of the self-purification of river waters of organic matter by the action of the oxygen contained in them, etc.

The conclusions of Pasteur were taken up by other chemists and observers and applied directly to the sewage disposal problem, and there are a number of opinions, based on experiment, to show that the organic matter of sewage is not oxidized upon being turned into a river, but is precipitated to the bottom or carried in solution.

Dr. Tidy.

Those opposed to the conclusions of Pasteur and other authorities have not been without support amongst scientific men, and it was attempted to be shown that instances did exist where river waters purified themselves of organic matter held by them, that such action was due to the oxidation of such matter, and hence that all rivers being subject to the same general influence of air, should so become purified.

Dr. Tidy, speaking of the clarification of the waters of the river Shannon, and loss of organic peaty matter in flowing short distances, says that "the quantity of organic matter (of peaty origin) is kept in check by the following means, which are two, namely:

"1. The inherent power that water possesses of self-purification "from the oxidation of the peat by the oxygen held in solution in the "water. This process is enormously helped by certain natural and "physical conditions, whereby the more complete aeration of the "water and the more intimate contact between oxygen and the peat is "effected.

" 2. Mechanical precipitation by admixture with coarse mineral "suspended matter." *("Tidy on River Water," Jour. Chem. Soc., vol. XXXVII, p. 295.)*

Frankland and Halcrow.

As offsetting this evidence of Dr. Tidy's, in favor of the self-purification theory, *Dr. Frankland* and *Miss Lucy Halcrow* conducted a series of experiments which " lead to the conclu-"sion that if peaty matter dissolved in river water is sponta-"neously oxidized at all (of which they consider there is no "sufficient proof), the process takes place with exceeding slow-"ness, and cannot be accomplished to any considerable extent, "in the flow of a river. The evidence proved the fact that "peaty matter is less oxidizable than animal matters under "the same conditions." (Halcrow and Frankland's tests of Tidy's conclusions, *Jour. of the Chem. Soc.*, vol. xxxvii, p. 506, Trans.)

Dr. Frankland, criticising Dr. Tidy's experiments, remarks that "the apparently superior action that Dr. Tidy attributes to air acting on" (the organic matter in) "running water" "is absent in the case" of water falling elsewhere than in the river channel. *("On the spontaneous oxidation of organic matter in water,"* Work cited, p. 538.)

Dr. Frankland has shown "that a flow of between 11 and 13 miles "of a stream polluted with sewage has very little effect on the organic "matter dissolved in the water even at a temperature of 18° Cent."

"And he has shown in the case of the River Wear, flowing between "Bishop Aukland and Durham, which has been quoted by Dr. Tidy

"in illustration of· his theory of oxidation of sewage, the purification
"is caused by an admixture of highly ferruginous waters, a fact which
"does not appear in Dr. Tidy's quotation."*

The above is an illustration of the class of error into which
some scientific men have fallen in this field of investigation,
and the subsequent exposure of such error by other investigations more thoroughly conducted.

But the investigation has been recently carried further and
evidence is now at hand which seems to set aside the strongest
argument of those who have held to the old theory—the argument of facts observed of the self-purification of peaty rivers.

Hartley and Kinahan's Experiments.

Mr. Gerard A. Kinahan, Association Royal College of
Science, Dublin, by and with the advice and consultation of
Prof. W. N. Hartley, F.R.S.E., has made a most satisfactory
study:—

1st—Of the effect of thorough aeration on the organic
peaty matter in river waters.

2d—Of the cause of the natural clearing of the waters of
some peaty rivers and loss of organic matter. (See *"Report on
the clearing of peaty waters,"* by Gerard A. Kinahan, 2d series,
Vol. III, Proc. Roy. Irish Academy, pp. 447, 596. Also, " *The
self-purification of peaty rivers,"* by W. N. Hartley, F.R.S.E.,
Jour. Soc. of Arts, 1882.)

Aeration does not produce oxidation.

Waters highly charged with organic peaty matter which in
their natural courses were dashed to spray in falling several
hundred feet (360 in one instance and 700 in another) in rock
bound channels in their natural course, being thus thoroughly
aerated, were found, as shown by analytical testing of the carbon, nitrogen, and ammonia contained therein, to have lost no
appreciable part of such organic matter.

Prof. Hartley says of these results: " I consider the fore-

---

* " *On the Self Purification of Peaty Rivers,*" by W. N. Hartley, F.R.S.E., *Journal Society of
Arts*, 1883.

"going analyses conclusive evidence that a peaty river cannot "undergo the slightest degree of purification from its organic "constituents by the natural process of aeration."

Mechanical Action.

The mechanical action of clay sand, pure quartzose sand, gelatinous silicia and magnesia, in reducing the amount of organic peaty matter by subsidence, was tested, but no reduction thereby could be detected.

The same action of carbonate of lime, powdered chalk, and limestone was found to be practically nothing, but the chemical action was slightly apparent in reducing the amount of organic matter.

In the same mechanical way the effect of particles of clay of different kinds was tested and found to be nothing, while the action of iron and alumina associated with these particles had some material effect on the peat coloring matter in causing the particles to adhere to the particles of clay "as to a mordant."

Professor Hartley says of this series of experiments :

"The results of the experiments with clay sand, pure quartzose "sand, gelatinous silicia, and magnesia, prove that there is no decol-"orizing action on the peaty coloring matter which can be described "as *mechanical.*"

Effect of Mineral Waters.

The effect of waters containing mineral matter in solution was tested where a tributary from a mining district, whose waters were highly charged with such mineral matters as ferric oxide, alumina, and copper, mingled with the waters of a peaty river, and it was found "that with the increase in min-"eral matter there was a marked decrease in the organic peaty "matter held in solution."

Effect of Low Temperature.

It was found that low temperatures caused the concentration of peaty coloring matters towards the bottom of a vessel and the clarification of that above; but the action was *very slight* in producing a precipitation of the peaty matter in the form of an insoluble sediment.

Peaty streams are less highly colored in cold weather, because the bogs are frozen and the waters run over instead of percolating through.

Oxides, etc.

Commonly occurring forms of metallic hydroxides—such as aluminic hydroxide and ferric hydroxide—caused a rapid and efficient precipitation of the coloring matter of peat waters, while the oxides of these waters were efficient but much less rapid in producing the same effect.

Chemical Action of Clays.

The chemical action of several kinds of clays, or their mineral constituents, in causing the precipitation of organic peaty matter from river waters was found to be very marked and prompt.

Peaty waters running in their natural beds are shown to be clarified by coming in contact with beds of blue clay, and by an admixture of iron stained waters flowing into them from marshy spots on their course—the iron " causing ochreous precipitations of peaty matter " " on to the stones of the channel," and " the waters becoming beautifully clear."

Professor Hartley says:

" This is a true case of the self-purification of a river water by the " action of a mineral constituent contained in its bed and banks."

Finally, the observations of Mr. Kinahan, and work of Prof. Hartley, have shown that the diminution in organic peaty matter observed and shown by Dr. Tidy to take place in the waters of the Shannon, is not caused by oxidation consequent upon aeration; "but is nothing more than the mixing of two " waters followed by the precipitation of organic matter con- " tained in one of them."

The results of the series of experiments undertaken by Prof. Hartley and Mr. Kinahan, although not altogether appli-

3

18

cable to the question of sewage pollution of river waters, when taken in connection with the outcome of the researches of Pasteur and of Frankland, seem to upset the arguments of Dr. Tidy, who has been one of the ablest defenders of the old theory of self-purification of river waters.

Mr. Folkard.

One of the very latest writers on this subject is *Mr. C. W. Folkard,* C. E., associate of the Royal School of Mines, member of the Institution of Civil Engineers. In 1882 he read a paper before the Institution, from which the following extracts and summarizations are made:

" Rivers are the natural drains of a country, into which every par-"ticle of rain falling within their watersheds (except, etc.,) ulti "mately finds its way, with everything which it is capable of dissolv-"ing or suspending. Highly manured arable lands, pastures, with "their thousands of cattle and sheep, mills, factories, village cess-"pools, and lastly town sewers, all contribute their quota of foul "water; in some cases to such an extent that the river becomes an "open sewer in which no fish can live, and the exhalations from "which, especially in hot climates, spread fever and death around."

Speaking of the detection of impurities in waters contaminated by sewage, Mr. Folkard says:

"The organic substances in solution and suspension are the most "important on account of their dangerous nature, and, unfortunately, "they are the ones with which the chemist is least able to deal. As "yet he has been compelled to be content with the examination and "estimation of the products of their decomposition—ammonia and "nitrous or nitric acids—or with the determination of one or two of "their constitutional elements (carbon and nitrogen)."

It is perhaps needless to say that these "organic substances" are contributed to sewage principally as the wastes of the human system.

Mr. Folkard asserts that in the matter of detecting organic impurities in water, chemists as yet are—

" Powerless to help the sanitarian in discriminating between whole-"some and unwholesome water." * * * * *
* * "In the first place," he says, "it is an ascertained fact, "proved beyond the possibility of doubt," (by microscopical methods),

"that mere dilution, however far soever it be carried, does not render
"inoperative the specific action of living germs."

The generally accepted theory of the propagation of *zymotic*
diseases is that the living germ, or matter capable of evolving
that germ under favorable conditions, being taken into the
system, such germs are propagated in the blood, and hence
the disease. Evidently in view of this theory, Mr. Folkard
says:

"Provided the individual is sufficiently weakly or unhealthy, it is
"of small importance whether he receive one thousand or one million
"parts of infectious matter (whether in the form of organized germs,
"or not, is immaterial), and, consequently, one part of infected sewage
"containing the dejecta of persons suffering from zymotic disease,
"mixed with one million parts of water, will be nearly as dangerous
"to him as one part per thousand."

The difference being simply, of course, the less chance there
would be of happening to drink the particular drop of water
carrying the germ matter when the rate of dilution is great
than when it is small ; and, also, again to use the words of our
authority, "the less contaminated water would probably not
affect a person in more robust health who might succumb to
the use of the highly contaminated sample."

This author insists "that it will be impossible to banish
"zymotic disease from a town where water supply has been con-
"taminated with the dejecta of patients suffering from that class
"of disease. The very weakly will contract it from the almost
"inappreciable amount of infection contained in the water, and
"from them it will spread to those who have resisted the poison
"in its diluted state."

He then goes on to state, as a conclusively established fact,
"that the germs which cause or accompany disease are en-
"dowed with the most persistent vitality, and are capable of
"withstanding heat, cold, moisture, drought, and even chemical
"agents, to a marvelous extent."

And illustrating this fact, he says :

"So difficult is it to destroy them that for many years the now ex-

" ploded doctrine of spontaneous generation found talented supporters
" who relied on their own carefully conducted experiments to prove
" the theory, all which experiments were subsequently found to have
" been rendered illusory by the astounding vitality of these low forms
" of life."

And finally upon this point, Mr. Folkard says :

" The conclusion, that, once contaminated, water never purifies
" itself sufficiently to be safe for dietetic purposes, becomes inevitable.
" * * * * The only safe test of the wholesomeness of a given water
" is by tracing it to its source, and ascertaining that no objectionable
" impurities gain access to it."

Emphasizing the conclusion that the waters of a running
stream once polluted with the class of matter of which I have
spoken, do not purify themselves, Mr. Folkard says:

" The chemist in the laboratory can effect complete purification
" only by adopting a similar process to that by which it is effected in
" nature—fixation of the ammonia in the soil, or its oxidation to
" nitric acid" (by the effect of contact with air or free oxygen), " fol-
" lowed by distillation by the heat of the sun."

He then gives an illustration of the effect of contributing
sewage matter, even in very small quantities, indeed—containing the dejecta of zymotic patients—upon the potable quality
of water, and says:

" The above is no fanciful picture. The experiment was tried on
" the inhabitants of a town in Surrey, unwittingly, it is true, but on
" that account the result is the more reliable. An epidemic broke
" out, and the consequent ·investigation revealed the cause in all its
" loathsome details. Fortunately for mankind at large, the relation
" in this case between cause and effect was distinctly traceable, but
" in the great majority of cases this is out of the question."

And finally, under this heading I find this unqualified conclusion :

" There is not the least evidence to show that foul water is ren-
" dered wholesome by flowing fifty or one hundred miles ; indeed,
" all experiments point in the opposite direction, on account of the
" persistent vitality of the organisms which accompany zymotic dis-
" ease, and of the utter failure of dilution to disarm these potent
" germs of corruption and death."

Mr. Folkard is of opinion that the sources of the pollution of river waters, besides town sewage, in England, are so numerous and varied in character, that they cannot be cut off, and, consequently, that the endeavor to purify such river waters so as to be fit for drinking purposes, by the exclusion of sewage from them, is futile; that the rivers ought to be abandoned as sources of water supply, and water stored or drawn from artesian wells be used altogether for drinking purposes.

Engineers Generally.

Engineers and sanitarians generally in England differ from him in this opinion, and show pretty conclusively that he is wrong on this point; but however this may be, any application of his theory to the conclusion that things should be let to drift as they are because they cannot be wholly remedied, is a weak point in argument even for the case as it stands in England, and no point at all in any argument which might come up on this matter in California. For our streams are not yet polluted to any considerable extent in the way we are now considering, and in the great central valley of the State, at least, the topography is such as to shield them from natural pollution to a very considerable extent. Our question here will be—shall the streams be preserved from pollution, so that the argument of bad-any-how-might-as-well-be-worse can never be used in opposition to proper sanitary measures.

Furthermore, this argument in favor of letting things drift as custom tends is answered by invoking the doctrine of chances brought forward by Mr. Folkard himself for the purpose of parts of his argument. The chances of bad results are greater in proportion to the certainty of pollution. That is to say, waters directly polluted from the zymotic patient by leading sewage into them are much more certain to prove poisonous to persons drinking them than waters which may have been polluted with the same class of noxious matter carried into them by the washings from streets, alleys, cow yards, manured fields, etc.

In the discussion before the Institution of Civil Engineers which followed the reading of Mr. Folkard's paper there were eminent men of learning and observation who differed with him upon some of his leading conclusions, as well as others who coincided with him in his views.

Baldwin Latham.

For instance: Mr. Baldwin Latham, a civil engineer of wide experience and special practice in sanitary works, maintained that there was evidence to show that river waters receiving sewage purified themselves of their organic disease germs in running less than the 50 to 100 miles of which Mr. Folkard spoke, and he cited the case of Birmingham, where there was no cholera in 1848–49, taking its waters for domestic use from the River Tame 20 miles down stream from where they were polluted by the sewage of Bilston, Wolverhampton, and other places where the disease raged violently.

Disease Propagation.

If I mistake not, however, the force of argument from this instance would be set aside by the recent, perhaps more recently adopted, theory of the germ-in-air propagation of this particular disease, and the conclusion that the action of the atmosphere being required to develop its germs the disease may not be conveyed in water charged with the dejecta of cholera patients.

However this may be though, and notwithstanding the fact that there is some evidence that poison is not always conveyed by means of waters polluted at localities where zymotic diseases prevail to quarters where the waters are used for domestic purposes, and notwithstanding the fact that there are still some men of attainment and observation in sanitary matters who contend that the deposit of sewage in running streams is not very dangerous to health and comfort, but that the waters purify themselves of the disease producing matters which have been put into them, as they advance on their course, in the literature of the subject, there are many more instances cited which appear to prove that disease is conveyed to great distances in running water; and, as I have said, the greater number of sanitarians—including engineers, doctors of medicine, chemists, microscopists, and biologists of eminence, and practical observers not of scientific attainment—so far as I am able to judge by a somewhat extended search and reading of the original authorities, now, either in moderate or in radically positive terms condemn the practice of polluting the waters of running streams even in a very slight degree by the introduction of crude sewage or any other similar matter therein.

The fact that a general practice yet is to dispose of the sewage of towns in this way is no argument in its favor or against the conclusion that it is a vile and filthy practice, unworthy of the age, and productive of a vast amount of misery and death to the people.

A very general practice, to this day, is to dispose of the noxious offal of dwellings in unlined pits that are never cleaned out, situated on the same village or town lot whence drinking waters are drawn from shallow surface wells ; yet no fact of sanitary science is more conclusively proven than that the soil, for considerable distances around such pits, is impregnated with the matter cast into them, and that the waters, even those found below an apparently impervious "hardpan" substratum, are polluted by contamination, and, being used as potable waters, are frequently the cause of diseases of the class ranked as *zymotic*, and which are so fatal.

These subjects are not thoroughly understood by sanitarians, in their several specialties even. There are undoubtedly remarkable exceptions to be noted, as I have before said, to the rule that impregnated waters carry disease germs great distances, and do not purify themselves ; but in explanation of these apparent exceptions, it is to be remembered : *First,* that they are in cases where cholera was not produced by the cause spoken of, and now it transpires that cholera is not conveyed in the water, but in the air, and : *Second,* that although disease may be shown not to have followed the drinking of waters polluted by its germs at a distance of twenty miles or more away in certain instances, this may not be evidence that the germs have been destroyed in the interim, but that the conditions necessary for their development in the persons of the population where imbibed, may not have been present.

And, finally, we have in explanation of these exceptional cases, the results of the most recent investigations, elsewhere given, which show that local causes, not general, *sometimes* purify river waters, but that these cases are rare.

The Difference of Opinion.

As accounting in a great degree for the difference of opinion on this subject in the countries where it has been forced to the public attention, we are to remember that the move to stop the pollution of the streams is a reform, a reform against an established abuse that has gradually grown up, that there are vast moneyed interests arrayed from selfish motives against the reform on the one side of the argument, while on the other side are those actuated purely by a love of truth, science, and cleanliness, and an interest in the welfare of the people at large.

If anything, England is a manufacturing country. Her vast wealth is largely invested in manufacturing establishments or enterprises connected therewith or dependent thereon. Manufactories of some kinds produce vast quantities of sewage matter. Paper mills, cotton, cloth, and woolen mills, bleaching establishments, dye works, chemical works, gas works, and a number of others being about the most prolific of such putrescible offal waters and wastes calculated to pollute waters and poison river beds and banks.

The manufacturers are a most powerful class; they are organized much as the hydraulic miners are in this State. Leading members of Parliament in both houses are said to be Manufacturing Kings. If this be so, and we can well believe a good deal of it, we have an explanation of the fact that the reform movement has made but slow progress in that country, and we have an explanation of the condition of things depicted in the following paragraph:

" It would really seem that although the whole country is agreed
" that the death rate is sensibly increased by neglecting the condition
" of our streams, no government is strong enough to revert to the
" law of the Egyptians and say: 'Thou shalt not defile our rivers.'
" Loss of life would appear to be preferred to loss of trade, and
" although the preference may be reconciled to *individual* interest, it
" is entirely opposed to the *national* weal." (Bailey Denton, Lectures,
etc., p. 47.)

And again (p. 181):

" The influence of the opposition of manufacturers upon the past
" and present governments has resulted in a temporary respite, and
" some ground has been lost by temporizing, which had been pre-
" viously gained by slow and steady steps; but when saying this it is
" impossible to evade the conclusion that the perfect and permanent
" cleansing of sewage will be sooner or later insisted upon by every
" voice in the country, and by no persons more decidedly than by
" the manufacturers themselves."

In closing this subject, notice of two leading opinions in our
own country will not be amiss, although they are not so late
in date as much which I have given above.

J. P. Kirkwood, C. E.

In 1875 the Legislature of the State of Massachusetts
enacted a law "*to provide for an investigation of the question of
the use of running streams as common sewers in its relation to
the public health.*"

By this law the. State Board of Health was instructed to
carry on themselves, or through their agents, an investigation
of the subject of "the correct method of drainage and sewerage
" of the cities and towns of the commonwealth, especially with
" regard to the pollution of the rivers, estuaries, and ponds by
" such drainage or sewerage."

On this general point condemnatory of the practice of
depositing sewage in the streams, Mr. James P. Kirkwood,
C. E., said:

"The maintenance of the purity of our running streams has been,
" in the United States, generally neglected.   *   *   *   *
" It was long thought that sewage was destroyed by running water,
" but now it is believed by chemists to be all but indestructible there."
*   *   *   *   *   *   *   *   *   *

4

"The poisons may be so largely diluted as to be beyond the read-
"ings of analysis, and yet they may be sufficient, when fairly pre-
"sented and understood, to render the water, by reason of that
"knowledge, not merely repulsive or suspicious, but more or less dan-
"gerous for family use." (Rept. Mass. Bd. of H., 1876, pp. 23–154.)

Mr. Kirkwood is a Civil Engineer of Brooklyn, N. Y., of
high standing, and the Board, in their report, say of him:
"Mr. Kirkwood has brought to the work a rare experience
"and a thorough knowledge of sanitary engineering. His
"conclusions and suggestions are fully concurred in by the
"Board." (Work cited, p. 9.)

In the report above cited is a paper by C. F. Folsom, M. D.,
Secretary of the Board, who in 1876 investigated the matter
of sewage disposal in Europe, and writes concerning that part
of the subject, and therein occurs the following:

"Much indeed has been said as to the complete self-purification of
"rivers by a flow of a few dozen miles. No such power exists. The
"solid parts are deposited, and what remains looks clear and bright,
"especially when largely diluted. Chemical changes take place too—
"sometimes decomposition, sometimes putrefaction, sometimes simple
"elective combinations. If sewage contain the germs of disease,
"whatever they may be, no agency at present known, except a suffi-
"ciently high temperature, will efficiently destroy them. Excessive
"dilution simply diminishes the chances of danger from any particular
"tumblerfull."

Without attempting to be at all thorough, for the subject
grows upon one's hands the further it is examined, I have
endeavored to show in this part of my report, by citing the
opinions and conclusions of those who have looked into the
subject in a thorough manner:

That house and town sewage is a noxious matter capable of
imparting or causing the most deadly diseases when taken
into the system in very moderate quantities even;

That deposited in a river, estuary, or other body of water
(except the sea, perhaps), it is not deprived of its noxious
qualities—*it is not destroyed, but diluted;*

That streams so polluted do not "purify themselves," that
the sewage is not "carried away" even, but that the solid

matters of the sewage settle to the bottom and there poison the soil of the channel bed and banks, and that much animal organic matter (supposed to be the germs of disease, or associated with such germs, or capable of evolving them, or of producing conditions under which disease is evolved, it matters not which), is held in solution in the water and is only *very slowly* destroyed;

And, hence, that any pollution of a stream by sewage matter is a *material* pollution;

That public opinion is being formed to these conclusions in older countries, but that the question is lulled to rest there and hushed up, and the reform in sewage disposal is only gradually progressing, because of the great outlay in works of sewerage already constructed having river outfalls, the consequent great expense to change the systems, and the immense moneyed interests in other ways arrayed from selfish motives against the reform;

And, finally, that any authority undertaking to dispose of sewage by depositing it in a stream, even one whose waters are but occasionally used and by a small number of people only, are assuming a responsibility or committing an act for which they may, in the near future, and certainly will, before many years go by, in some form, be held accountable, at least, as having erred.

If I have failed in adducing evidence to substantiate these views, it may be said that I have not done the subject justice in my selection and arrangement of it, for enough may be had to make this report many times as long as it is, and from the best sources, and of the most practical kind.

WHAT SHALL BE DONE WITH SEWAGE?

"LAND THE PURIFIER OF LIQUID SEWAGE."

The sewage of which we speak, as I have before written, is polluted water—the proportion of polluting matter being small as compared to that of the water; and the object of all sewerage work should be to dispose of the noxious matter so that at least it may do no harm, if, indeed, it be not made useful, and to restore the water to a state approximating purity.

Cultivated land is the natural, as it is the best, practicable medium for the purification of the noxious matters which pollute the waters of sewage.

Land of suitable soil, properly prepared, with the environments of locality and climate favorable, affords, to judicious use, all of the essential conditions under which the chemical changes necessary for the purification of sewage waters take place, in the most presentable form for the purpose, that we can hope to find in practice.

The Action of Soil and Air.

The immediate object to be held in view is to prevent decomposition or arrest fermentation of the organic matters contained in the sewage, and thus forestall the development of organic germs, or the conditions under which they may be developed, and the giving off of foul odors.

Moisture to saturation being an essential condition to this process of decomposition or fermentation, and subsequent development, the removal of such excessive moisture deprives the matter of the environment necessary to the baneful action.

And again, the action of the air upon the particles of matter is essential to the rapid change which it is desired to produce, and dispersion or separation of these particles is essential to the free access of the air.

In applying sewage to land, then, under the conditions and in the manner heretofore spoken of as most favorable to a successful issue, the exact conditions are produced which best admit of those natural actions which we want to help along; the putrescible particles are arrested in their course or adhere to the granules of earth which absorb the moisture from them, thus arresting decomposition, and hold them subject to the action of the air, thus effecting their oxidation; and finally, vegetation afterwards assimilates the resultant matters, and so the change becomes complete.

Conditions Essential to Success.

From these considerations we see at once that conditions essential to the efficiency of this mode of disposing of sewage are a free, absorbing, and well aerated soil, or, at least, in each case, an application of sewage not in excess of the capacity of the soil, freely and promptly to absorb or take into its pores the liquid and suspended solid matters, without resulting in complete saturation and without leaving a considerable scum or precipitate on the surface, at least a fair depth to the soil, and such under-drainage, natural or artificial, as will promptly lead away superfluous moisture and produce aeration of the soil; and, finally, cultivation of the soil and plant growth thereon at least annually on at not distant intervals.

Some Authorities.

As I have before written, this question of sewage disposal has attracted a great deal of attention in England, and has been the subject of a number of practical and scientific investigations and inquiries, carried out under authority of law, or under the patronage or guidance of societies of arts or science.

Without exception, so far as my examination goes, and I have diligently traced the course of these inquiries in the original reports or publications, wherever the question of the disposal of sewage has been the one at issue and it has been fairly met, the conclusion arrived at by such inquiries has been either unqualifiedly in favor of irrigation in all cases *where possible*, or in all cases *where convenient*.

I have been unable to find one authoritative verdict against it. Differences of opinion are only in the degree of favor shown it, or as to the necessity of precipitating the solid matter before using the liquid on the land, or as to the area of land necessary for a fixed amount of sewage, and as to the economy of the plan of disposal—taking into account the high price of land and other complicating circumstances.

Land the Proper Purifier.

I present here a few of the many unqualified decisions upon which the views I have advanced have been founded. Selecting only those which come from some authoritative or specially high source, I remark that individual opinions of civil engineers, sanitarians, chemists of high standing, and town authorities might be quoted by the chapter, which coincide with them.

First come some authoritative opinions as to the efficiency of irrigation as a means of disposal of sewage.

The Sewage of Towns Commission.

The Sewage of Towns Commissioners of England in their first report (1858) showed that they considered that the irrigation of land (in some cases supplemented by other processes) was the best means of preventing the pollution of streams by sewage.

And in their third report (1865), p. 3, they state in the most emphatic terms that "the right way to dispose of town sewage " is to apply it continually to land, and it is only by such " application that the pollution of rivers can be avoided." (*Corfield*, "Treatment and Utilization of Sewage," p. 231.)

The First Rivers Pollution Commission.

The First Rivers Pollution Commissioners, in their third report, submit the following as a conviction arrived at by them after their extensive and thorough inquiry into the subject, " that the right way to dispose of town sewage is to apply it " continually to land, and it is only by such application that " the pollution of rivers can be avoided."

The Local Government Board Sewage Committee.

The Committee of the Local Government Board on Sewage Disposal, in their report of 1876, indorse the above conclusion of the Rivers' Pollution Commission in favor of irrigation, saying : "They (the conclusions) have as much value now as at the time when made" (p. 116). And as one of their own convictions they say, "that town sewage can best and most " cheaply be disposed of and purified by the process of land " irrigation for agricultural purposes, when local conditions " are favorable to its application " (p. xiii of report).

Ex. Com. Society of Arts Conference, 1876.

The Executive Committee of the Society of Arts Conference, in summing up the results which seemed to them to have been established by that extended and interesting inquiry and discussion, give precedence to *irrigation* as the best means of purifying sewage, in the following words :

"(1) In certain localities, where land at a reasonable price can " be procured with favorable natural gradients, with soil of a suitable " quality and in sufficient quantity, a sewage farm, if properly con- " ducted, is apparently the best method of disposing of water-carried " sewage." (Jour. Soc. of Arts, vol. xxiv, p. 737, June 16, 1876.)

In 1862 a committee was appointed by resolution of Parliament to examine this matter, take testimony, and report. It was called the "Select Committee on the Sewage of Towns." The conclusions arrived at by this committee are so very instructive and pointed that I present them entire :

" 1. The evidence proves that sewage contains the elements of " every crop which is grown.

" 2. That as compared with solid manure there are advantages in
" the application of sewage manure to land.

" 3. The evidence proves that town sewage contains a large amount
" of heat, which in itself is beneficial in stimulating vegetation.

" 4. The evidence further proves that one ton (224 gallons) of
" average town sewage contains an amount of manure which, if ex-
" tracted and dried, would be worth a little over 2d., taking Peruvian
" guano (at 11s. per ton as the standard).

" 6. A judicious use of town sewage permanently improves land.

" 7. Sewage may be applied to common grass, Italian rye-grass,
" and also to roots and grain crops with great advantage, dressings
" with sewage hastening vegetation.

" 8. Sewage-grown grass has a great effect in increasing the quan-
" tity and richness of the milk of cows, as well as improving the con-
" dition of the cattle, which prefer sewaged grass to all others.

" 9. The earth possesses the power of absorbing from sewage all
" the manure which it contains, if the dressings in volume are pro-
" portioned to the depth and quality of the soil.

" 10. Those who use sewage should have full control over it, that
" they may apply it when and in what quantities they may require it.

" 11. Heavy dressings of sewage (8,000 to 9,000 tons per acre),
" are wasteful; less dressings (500 to 2,000 tons per acre), when more
" carefully applied, produce better results. The enormous dressings
" recommended by some witnesses would be agriculturally useless, as
" the sewage would flow over and off the surface unchanged.

" 12. When the sewage of our cities, towns, and villages is utilized
" to the best advantage over suitable areas, little or no imported or
" manufactured manures would be required in such districts.

" 13. Sewage may be applied with advantage to every description
" of soil which is naturally or artificially drained.

" 14. The most profitable returns, as in the case of all other
" manures, will be obtained when sewage is judiciously applied to the
" best class of soils.

" 15. Sewage may be advantageously applied to land throughout
" the entire year.

" 16. Some matters used in manufactures which enter town sewers,
" such as waste acids, would be in themselves injurious if applied to
" vegetation; but bearing as they do so small a proportion to the
" entire volume of sewage into which they are turned, they are ren-
" dered harmless.

" 17. Fresh sewage at the outfall of the sewers, even in the hot-
" test weather, is very slightly offensive; and if applied to the land in
" this state in such dressings as can at once be absorbed by the earth,
" fear of nuisance need not be felt, as the soil possesses the power to
" deodorise and separate from liquids all the manure which they
" contain.

" 18. Large dressings and an overtaxed soil may pollute surface
" streams, subsoils, and shallow wells.

" 19. Solid manure cannot be manufactured from town sewage
" with commercially profitable results."

The Massachusetts State Board of Health.

The Massachusetts State Board of Health, at the close of a most extended report on the whole sewage question, covering upwards of four hundred pages, made after careful research by men of ability—one of whom, Dr. C. F. Folsom, made an extended trip to Europe for the purpose of studying the question—advance, as a primary recommendation, the following :

"I. That no city or town shall be allowed to discharge sewage " into any watercourse or pond, without first purifying it according to " the best process at present known, and which consists in irriga-
" tion," etc.   *   *   *   *   *   *   *   *   *
"VI. That irrigation be adopted, at first experimentally, in those " places where some process of purification of sewage is necessary ; " and that cities and towns be authorized by law to take such land " as may be necessary for the purpose."

And they say, before advancing this recommendation, that :

"In public institutions, prisons, asylums, etc., it is our opinion " that the sewage can be utilized and purified by irrigation to great " advantage, and this disposal of it should be made when the land " can be got."

The First Rivers Pollution Commission, in their report, 1867, said :

"Sewage interception is always practical. Where it can be applied " fresh to land there is least nuisance, and least cost to the rate " payers.   *   *   *   *   *   *   *   No arrangements for treating " sewage are satisfactory, except its direct application to land for agri-
" cultural purposes."

Speaking of this opinion, Dr. Folsom writes :

"This statement may fairly be taken as the result of twenty-five " years' experience in England" (that is, previous to 1867) ; "and " the 'official opinion,' if the term may be used, has not changed " since that time." (Down to 1876.)   *   *   *   *   "No authori-
" tative body, so far as I have been able to learn, has declared itself " as fully satisfied with any other process for the purification of sew-
" age than that of irrigation." (Rept. Mass. State Bd. of H., 1876, p. 299.)

Sanitary Influence of a Sewage Farm.

Lands irrigated with sewage are not productive of sickness to the residents upon them or in their neighborhood, as is attested by the following evidence, culled from a great mass to the same effect, scattered through many official documents, and, so far as I have been able to find, there is no authoritative evidence to the contrary.

The First Rivers Pollution Commission.

The Rivers Pollution Commissioners, in their first report, say :

"We do not recommend irrigation for the abatement of the town " sewage nuisance without having made ample inquiry into any risk " to health which may be incurred by the establishment of sewage " meadows in the neighborhood of towns. Such inquiries have been " made at Edinburgh, Croydon, Norwood, and Barking, where irri- " gation has been carried on long enough and, near Edinburgh, at " least, in a sufficiently careless manner to have certainly developed " whatever elements of mischief may be inherent in the practice. " Nowhere have we found instances of ill health that are properly " attributable to malaria or other causes due to irrigation."

Dr. Littlejohn, Medical Officer of Health to Edinburgh, in evidence before the Commission, said he entertained a prejudice against the maintenance of sewage meadows so near the city, but that he had not been able to connect any ill health of the city with the meadows as its cause.

Professor Christison, President of the Royal Society of Edinburgh, speaking of these meadows, in an address at the meeting of the Association for the Encouragement of Social Science at Edinburgh, in October, 1863, said :

" Many years ago my own prejudices were all against the meadows; " I have been compelled to surrender them. I am satisfied that " neither typhus, nor enteric fever, nor dysentery, nor cholera, is to " be encountered in or around them, whether in epidemic or non- " epidemic seasons, more than in any other agricultural district of " the neighborhood."

He then gives certain facts ascertained by his investigation of the subject, upon which he has based his conclusion, and says : " I think it right, in reference to the late introduction of " the Craigentinny system of irrigation into the vicinity of " other large towns, that these precise facts should be known." In 1870, this Dr. Christison writes : " I have nothing either

"to add to or subtract from the above quotation from my
"Social Science address in 1863."

Then follows a mass of other evidence of like import from
men competent to observe closely and draw valuable conclusions, that was collected by the Commission, from which we
are bound to conclude that they could have come to no other
conclusion.

The Second Rivers Pollution Commission.

The fourth report of the Rivers Pollution Commission
made, be it remembered, by entirely different individuals, as
heretofore explained, contains further evidence and expression
of opinion to the same point.

Dr. Littlejohn again gives testimony with respect to
the healthfulness of the neighborhood of the Craigentinny
Meadows, and after speaking of the general good health of
the people of Restelrig, which is surrounded by these meadows,
he says :

"I expected that the first part of Edinburgh (Regent Terrace
"and Carleton Terrace, on the Calton Hill), against which the wind
"blowing over these meadows impinges, would have exhibited evi-
"dence of infection in the shape of cholera or typhoid fever, but I
" have totally failed to find it so."

Speaking of the health of the soldiers at the neighboring
barracks, he says: "No injurious effect is produced by the
"meadows which is perceptible in the state of their health."

The Commission say that there is no evidence of the meadows
producing ill health, and much to the effect that they do not
have any such influence.

It is to be remarked that these meadows are frequently
spoken of in the literature of sewage irrigation as an example of very careless management, and bad arrangement, and
that the air in their neighborhood is oftentimes very offensive
to the olfactory organs.

The Commission made particular inquiry as to the health of
cows fed upon sewage-produced grass from these meadows as
well as others, and in this fourth report I find amongst other

evidence on this point, the following from Dr. Littlejohn, the medical officer of health. He says:

" The cows in Edinburgh are chiefly fed with grass that is grown "on the Craigentinny Meadows. I have thought that there might " be objection to feeding cows upon grass so grown, because I was of "opinion that such grass might be of inferior quality; but practically " I have failed to detect any bad effects resulting from the use of such " grass."

He then goes on to specify at length the character of diseases he would have looked for, and speaks of their remarkable absence, as shown by inspection and dissection of the animals, closing with the following :

" The practice of keeping cows in Edinburgh has prevailed from "time immemorial. If there had been anything in the idea that "sewage grass would lead indirectly to entozoic disease, it has had "plenty of time to develop itself, and Edinburgh is not only the seat "of a great medical school, but medical observation is carried to the " highest point in Edinburgh, so that it could not fail of being detected."

Committee of the Royal Agricultural Society.

In 1879, two prizes, each of the value of one hundred pounds (sterling), were offered for the best managed sewage farms in England and Wales, by the Mansion House Committee, in connection with the London International Exhibition of the Society, and these prizes were accepted by the Council.

A committee, consisting of Mr. Baldwin Latham, civil engineer, Clare S. Read, and Thomas H. Thursfield, was appointed to examine the farms entered for the prizes, and their management, and report thereon.

The report of this committee is one of great interest and value, covering eighty pages octavo, closely printed matter. I take one extract for presentation here, hoping to embody in an appendix, at a future day, a summary of the practical information contained in this and other similar papers.

In concluding, the Committee say :

" With respect to the sanitary aspect of sewage farming, the above " table will show the several particulars which have been collected in

" reference to the farms during the period they have been in opera-
" tion, the number of persons either living or working on the farms,
" the number of children residing on the farms, and the number of
" deaths which have occurred.

"An examination of this table will show that the rate of mortality
" on an average of the number of years which these farms have been
" in operation does not exceed three per thousand per annum.   This
" is a very low rate, but in all probability it may not be lower
" than would be found in an equal number of selected lives taken
" from an agricultural district.   The results of the sanitary inquiry
" show that sewage farming is not detrimental to life or health."
*   *   *   *   *   *   *   *   *   *   *

" Sewage farming is becoming an important agricultural feature in
" the country, there being at the present time about one hundred
" such farms in operation." (Jour. Royal Agricultural Soc., vol. xvi,
2d series, pp. 1–80.)

This last testimony and opinion is important as being of
recent date, and the result of a systematic inquiry into the subject, from the agricultural standpoint.

I refrain from presenting more evidence on this point, because, with what is to be said hereafter about proper drainage,
this ought to be enough.

SOME AUTHORITIES.

Mr. Bailey Denton.

Mr. Bailey Denton, one of the oldest and first sanitary
engineers in Great Britain, in closing a series of lectures (the
printed reports of which cover 360 large octavo pages) delivered
at the Royal School of Military Engineering, at Chatham, in
1876, on the subject of sanitary engineering generally, draws
the first of twelve main conclusions in the following language:

"I. That the liquid refuse of towns, villages, hamlets, institutions,
"and dwellings, can only be continuously, effectually, and econom-
"ically cleansed and rendered legally admissible into inland rivers
"by application to land." (Work cited, p. 351.)

Then follows nine conclusions relating to the subject as presented in England—by the complications of high prices of
lands, numerous manufactories, sewerage works already constructed, rivers already polluted—which have no bearing to

our present case here, and then we come to the eleventh conclusion, which is as follows:

"XI. Land receiving sewage should be most carefully prepared to
"distribute it while in a fresh condition. All half and half measures
"result sooner or later in river pollution, and loss to the rate-payers."

And in speaking of land which is suitable for the reception
of sewage, he says: "Always assuming that it is naturally or
"artificially well underdrained."

Mr. C. N. Bazalgette.

In closing one of the most notable papers upon this *Sewage
Question* which has appeared of late years, and which was read
before the Institution of Civil Engineers, London, in 1877, the
author, Mr. Charles Normann Bazalgette, laid down as a
primary conclusion for the discussion of the Society, the following: "That where land can be reasonably acquired, irrigation is the best and most satisfactorily known system for the
disposal of sewage."

And in the course of his paper he says:

"In broad irrigation it is not merely the surface contact of the
"sewage with the soil assisted by the oxidizing influence of vegetation,
"which conduces to the resolution of sewage into its innocuous
"elements, but above all its passage through that aerated earth filter
"which intervenes between the surface and the subsoil (water) drain-
"age." (Minutes of the Proceedings of the Institution of Civil Engineers, Vol. XLIII, pp. 105–160.)

Mr. W. Crookes.

In discussing Mr. Bazalgette's paper, Mr. W. Crookes, one of
his principal opponents, "who, for some years, had made this
subject his special study," and who did not agree with Mr. B.
in others of his conclusions, nor fully even in this one, said:

"As a process which numbers many and most zealous—not to say
"occasionally intolerant—advocates, I first refer to irrigation. No one
"can dispute that earth has a wonderfully deodorizing power, which
"increases the more finely the soil is pulverized and subdivided, and
"the more thoroughly it gives passage to the air. The fœcal matters
"and other impurities attach themselves to the surfaces of the particles

"of earth by a kind of cohesive attraction, and in this state are readily
"attacked by the oxygen of the air. Their organic carbon becomes
"carbonic acid; their nitrogen is converted into nitrous or nitric acid,
"which unites with lime, magnesia, and other basic elements present."

He then goes on to speak of the unsuitableness of some kinds
of land, and the difficulty of securing land for this purpose in
many parts of England, together with the limited variety of
crops to which sewage waters can be advantageously applied,
and concludes, while admitting the efficiency and value of
irrigation as a process for the purification of sewage under
favorable circumstances, that, owing to the absence of these
circumstances in most cases, the method cannot be looked to
as one solving the sewage problem for England.

The original paper covers fifty-five closely printed octavo
pages, and considers the question from every standpoint, as a
review of the experience had and published up to that date.
The discussion which followed was participated in by a number
of engineers and scientists of good standing, the report of
which covers ninety similar pages; and the correspondence on
the subject, appearing in the following volume, covers forty-five
additional pages.

The opinions quoted above fairly represent those of the
participants in this discussion, so far as expressed on this head
of irrigation, the one being outspoken in favor of irrigation as
a means of disposal, and as probably the chief means to be
looked to in the country, the other scarcely less favorable to
irrigation in itself, but asserting it to be inapplicable in a great
majority of cases in England, because of peculiar local circumstances.

Prof. W. H. Corfield.

The most complete authority on the subject of sewage
purification, up to the time of its publication (1871), is the
work of Prof. Corfield. After an exhaustive review of the
subject, in which he collates a vast amount of evidence from
practical experience, a reading of which is most impressive, he
advances his chief conclusion in the following words:

"(a) That by careful and well conducted sewage irrigation,
"especially with the application of moderate quantities per acre, the
"purification of the whole liquid refuse of a town is practically per-
"fect, and has been insured in cases where it was not at all the object
"of the agriculturist; and that it is the only process known by which
"that purification can be effected on a large or on a small scale." (p.
270.)

And at the end of a chapter on the "Influence of Sewage
Farming on the Public Health," after adducing very interesting and pointed evidence to the effect that the health of people
living on and near sewage farms, so far from being bad or
worse than that of people in general living on agricultural
lands, is in notable cases better, the author says:

"We have good reason to expect that it will be found to be the
"case, that the utilization of the sewage of towns on the land
"near them, while preventing the pollution of drinking water, and
"the spread thereby of cholera and typhoid fever, will at the same
"time maintain the purity of the atmosphere around and about the
"town, and the result will be, especially when combined with that
"produced by the increased demand for labor and the more plentiful
"supply of food, a diminution of the general death-rate." (p. 283.)

CAUSES OF OPPOSITION TO IRRIGATION.

Where the use of sewage waters in irrigation has failed to
prove an efficient means of disposing of them, or of so far
purifying them as to render them as fit to be put into rivers as
the drainage waters from any highly cultivated, stocked, or
manured farm lands, it is asserted upon the highest authority,
and generally acceded to, that such result is due to one or
more of five causes:

The quality of sewage applied has been too great for the
land irrigated under the immediate and surrounding circumstances;

The soil of the land has been radically unsuited for the purpose, or it has not been properly prepared for such use;

The manner of application has been careless or from other
cause needlessly inefficient;

Sewage irrigation has been practiced on quite a large scale in England since about
1853, when the Rugby sewage farm was established. There are now upwards of
one hundred localities where towns and cities thus dispose of their drainage, and
the number is increasing rapidly.

The land has been kept continuously in use for sewage purification, without cultivation and growth of crops, for too long a period of time; or,

The sewage itself has been exceptionally foul and full of putrescible matter, and has not been treated or defecated before application to the land.

These Causes Might Operate Anywhere.

The above causes of failure are such as, without proper knowledge and care, are liable to recur at any point where irrigation is resorted to as a means of disposal and purification of sewage, and of course are to be guarded against in the selection and preparation of lands and the subsequent use thereof for the purpose.

I have already cited some authorities which bear on this point and will only call attention to one other: Mr. Baldwin Latham, an English civil engineer who has had much experience in sanitary work and written a work of merit on the subject, at a meeting of the Association of Sanitary Engineers held at Merton in 1879, speaking of the sewage disposal works at Croyden, where the sewage from a town of 17,000 people is put on to 28 acres of land for filtration, after the solid matter in suspension has been precipitated from it in tanks, said:

"In fact, if the sewage was not seen nobody would find fault with "it. The only objection he had found in treating sewage was entirely "one of sentiment. When people saw sewage, or knew it was near "them, they thought that there must be an offensive smell. He had "never found any great nuisance arising from a sewage farm if it was "only moderately well conducted." (Proceedings of the Association of Sanitary Engineers, Vol. VI, p. 104.)

We should remember that it is the solid matter in suspension and in solution which, being allowed to stand long enough, decomposes and becomes offensive; that earth is the best known agent to check this decomposition; that the water is the carrier, simply, of the other substances composing the sewage; that if the soil is supplied with this matter in proper quantity, and is *properly underdrained*, so that it does not at any time become water-logged, the result is simply an application of the particles liable to decomposition, to their natural deodorizer and disinfector—earth particles—there to be held, deodorized and disinfected for the action of the air in the soil to complete the work by oxidation.

Other Causes Peculiar to the Old Country.

In England and other parts of Europe the popular expectations from irrigation as a sewage treatment, has been disappointed in a number of cases, from causes of another nature. These causes being peculiar to the manner in which the subject was presented there, or to the social or political condition of the country, are not likely to recur here, and certainly will not if the subject is properly taken in hand when it should be, and not put off until we have a dense population.

England is a densely populated country; and land in the neighborhood of cities and towns has its prefixed uses or actual or prospective value, far in excess of that which obtains here.

So that it is difficult—sometimes almost impossible—to get sufficient land of suitable quality and favorably situated, to admit of the adoption of irrigation as a means of disposal of the sewage of many towns and cities in that country.

Intermittent Downward Filtration.

To avoid this embarrassment the process known as *intermittent downward filtration*, whereby lands were deeply underdrained and used more as filter beds than as cultivated tracts, with the view of disposing of a greater quantity of sewage upon the acre of land, was resorted to. It is alleged by one school of sanitarians that by this process the sewage of 1,500 people can be effectively disposed of, without nuisance, upon an acre of land, and it is claimed that in several places in England the practice runs as high as 1,000 persons per acre. Be this as it may, the principle is essentially the same as that of irrigation, with the absence, to a great extent, of the action of plant growth on the land, and I have found no evidence amongst the vast mass, pro and con, on the relative merits of *broad* (ordinary) *irrigation* and *intermittent downward filtration*, which inclines my judgment in favor of the latter under circumstances where land is to be had in abundance.

We must remember, then, that what is said against irrigation as a means of disposing of sewage in England is very largely on account of the difficulty of getting enough land for the purpose adjacent to the cities.   .

Climate of England Not Favorable.

Beyond this, the climate is not such as to make artificial irrigation, with any water, on a broad scale for agricultural purposes, either necessary or very desirable, except for the special purpose of forcing grass on meadows, and for this use sewage waters are not altogether well adapted ; and, furthermore, English farmers are not an irrigating people, and would not generally contemplate irrigation except for the necessity of disposing of sewage waters.

It will be seen at once that irrigation was undertaken there by reason of a motive engendered, as it were, outside of the necessities of agriculture—the irrigation was not demanded by the agricultural classes, but owing to the necessity under which the people living in towns rested, to dispose of their polluted waters, some agriculturists, from time to time, have been induced to undertake irrigation with sewage waters.

The Reform Movement.

Like all reforms, much more was claimed for this than it justly deserved.

It was claimed that sewage contained vast amounts of fertilizing matters, which being applied to lands would greatly increase their productive powers ; that farming with sewage would be exceedingly remunerative ; that the farmer should pay for the privilege of using the sewage ; and, hence, it would be a source of revenue to the community producing as well as to the farmer using it.

The facts (1) that there would be exceptional inconveniences and expenses attending its use; (2) that the fertilizing elements, although present in the sewage, were not and could not, without the lapse of time and under favorable conditions, be in a proper condition for assimilation as plant food; (3) that more land would be required for the application of the sewage as years rolled on, or, in other words, that lands should rest and be cultivated without the application of sewage for a season or two now and then ; (4) that all soils were not equally favorable for sewage reception, and some decidedly unfavorable, requiring considerable and skillful preparation to make them at all suited for such use ; (5) that more than an ordinary degree of skill, judgment, faith, and care would be required in the conduct of farming operations by the use of sewage ; (6) that all sewage is not alike, or that sewage from some towns— by reason principally of the manufacturing refuse and waste waters largely forming it—is in its crude state unfit for application to lands where cultivation is practiced, and sewage from other towns contains so much solid matter, or solid matter of such a character that the pores of the soil to which it applies become clogged ; (7) that comparatively few crops are suitable for cultivation by irrigation in the climate of England, and not all of these are suitable for growth upon lands constantly under irrigation with foul waters ; (8) that a very considerable prejudice existed amongst the laboring population to working on irrigated lands, and a greater prejudice against working on lands irrigated with highly polluted waters ; (9) that a very great prejudice existed against consuming the products resulting from the use of polluted waters ; and finally, (10) that municipal corporations cannot act to the same advantage in such matters as can private individuals—these facts, I say, were overlooked.

Experience has shown that only under exceptionally favorable circumstances—and these circumstances are many and

not often rightly combined—can anything more than the ordinary profit of farming be secured from the use of sewage in
irrigation *in Great Britain ;* and, hence, that the communities
producing the sewage cannot only not expect to derive a revenue
from it, but, generally speaking, must be at expense to assist
in handling it, in order that the farmer may be compensated
for the inconvenience to which he is put, or helped with the
extra labor necessitated by its use ; and, beyond this, it is found
advisable in some instances, where the available area of land
is restricted, or its soil not suitable, or the sewage is of a
specially noxious character, or for other reasons not necessary
here to be mentioned, to deprive the sewage waters of nearly
all the matter carried in suspension by them before application
is made to the land, thus involving the cost of works for the
treatment of the sewage and the expense of their maintenance
and operation, which, of course, falls upon the community
sewered.

The "Sludge" Complication.

And at this stage of the experience another sore disappoint-
ment, which has been general, made itself felt : It was repre-
sented, as an inducement to the municipalities to clarify their
sewage waters, that the resulting solid manure would be of

I have said that authorities generally concur in the opinion that the best way to
dispose of sewage is to apply it to land—that irrigation *per se* presents the only
satisfactory solution of the sewage disposal problem yet arrived at, and that in all
cases where an outfall into a *large* tidal estuary, or bay, or the sea, is not afforded,
irrigation should undoubtedly be resorted to when land, climate, and other circumstances are favorable. I say this, notwithstanding what is written by Mr. George
E. Waring in his "Sanitary Drainage of Houses and Towns," in the first two pages
of chapter ten, from which we might infer that authorities are not in any way settled
upon the efficiency of any method of sewage disposal.

In the first place, it is not clear that this author includes *irrigation* when he says
that "none of these schemes have so far achieved the success claimed for them, as
"to gain the confidence of the engineering world at large," but that he refers
exclusively to the various patented devices for purifying sewage by chemical and
mechanical means. In the next place, I read on and find him speaking of *irrigation* and the "*Coventry process*" as "one or two devices which seem to afford relief
"in the case of small villages, and especially of large or small establishments."
And, lastly, I take his book at his own estimate, to be found in the preface, as follows :
"The following chapters are not offered as of material value to such engineers
"and architects as have given attention to the subject, as these would naturally
"resort to the original authorities from which they have been so largely drawn.
"They are addressed more especially to the average citizen and householder, and
"are intended rather as an incentive to the securing of good work, than as a guide
"to the manner of its performance."

sufficient market value to more than cover the expense of the process, together with interest on the works. But this expectation also proved fallacious, as will be explained more fully in the next chapter of this report; and so it has transpired that irrigation is simply a method of purifying sewage waters, efficient in itself under ordinary conditions; that sewerage is a process of clearing filth from a town, and that "towns must pay to be clean," and cannot make capital out of their offal, at least not in England.

CONCLUSION.

In closing this part of my report, I call attention to the points which I have endeavored to make apparent, viz.:

That irrigation is the proper mode of disposing of sewage waters.

That their proper use on properly prepared lands does not produce an insanitary condition of the immediate neighborhood.

That by proper appliances and management, the neighborhood of a sewage irrigated field need not be even moderately offensive, but will be inoffensive.

That in climates suited for irrigation at all, sewage waters are valuable and ought not to be thrown away.

That opinions in older countries are almost unanimous as to the above mentioned points.

As I said, in closing the last part of this report, if my conclusions are not established by evidence, it is only because I have refrained from transcribing enough of the supply, or have not chosen well, or have not arranged well the parts chosen.

The facts are well proven and generally admitted.

WHAT SHALL BE DONE WITH SEWAGE?

PART III—ARTIFICIAL TREATMENT OF SEWAGE.

FILTRATION, PRECIPITATION, PURIFICATION.

In the two preceding chapters I have briefly sketched, in outline, the history of the sewage disposal problem in England and other older countries. We have seen the growing evil of rivers pollution, the outcry against it, the declaration that it was all a myth—that the waters purified themselves in running a short distance—the refutation of this fallacy, the fearless assertion of the most eminent men of science from disinterested motives, and in the face of the clamor of the great moneyed classes of the country (the landlords or "rate payers," and the manufacturers), that it was suicidal to put town sewage and manufacturing refuse into the streams of the country; and we have seen that the outcome of authoritative inquiry into the best means of disposing of sewage has repeatedly and uniformly been a conclusion declaring that it should be applied to land.

In the course of this review I have referred to the fact that many differences on the part of authorities were in degree only of opposition to the pollution of rivers by the deposit of sewage in them, and in degree of advocacy of the application of sewage to land, rather than the disputing of the opposition to the one or the advocacy of the other measure altogether, and I have spoken of means which, it had been asserted, reconciled the disputants. It remains now to consider these means.

The agitation against the practice of pollution of the rivers with sewage and manufacturing offal, taken up, as it was, by.

7

some of the most powerful associations and most accomplished individuals of England, was a very serious matter to many large moneyed interests in the country. The questions were carried into the Courts, and in most cases decided in · favor of the plaintiffs, and injunctions were issued restraining the town, or manufactory, as the case might be, from dumping its sewage into the stream.

THE LAND DIFFICULTY.

A way out of the difficulty was eagerly sought. In many cases it was impossible to get sufficient suitable land properly located for irrigation.

Cheltenham, *Gloucester*, in 1870, paid about $400 per acre for 131 acres of land, quite unsuitable in soil, upon which to run its sewage, and this was not more than one fourth as much land as was needed.

Bedford, *Bedfordshire*, pays $25 per year per acre for the use of land upon which to put sewage.

Bishops Stortford, *Hertfordshire*, paid about $340 per acre for ninety-seven acres for its sewage farm, and has to pump the sewage up to it.

Banbury, *Oxfordshire*, acting under the impulse of an injunction and order restraining the town from polluting the River Cherwell, in 1864, paid about $1,275 per acre for 100 acres upon which to put its sewage, and also has to pump the liquid on to the land.

Kendal, *Westmoreland*, in 1873, paid about $1,260 per acre for sixty-five acres upon which to dispose of its sewage.

Chorley, *Lancashire*, under an order of the Court of Chancery, to abstain from polluting the waters of the River Yarrow, in 1867, paid at the rate of about $400 per acre for eighty-seven acres and about $540 per acre for forty-six acres, composing its sewage irrigation farm.

West Derby, *Lancashire*, in 1875, paid at the rate of about $730 per acre for 207 acres upon which to dispose of its sewage. (Robinson & Mellis, p. 89, *et seq.*)

And so this list might be run out to almost a hundred places which, within the past fifteen or twenty years, most of them within the past ten years, have been forced by order of the Courts or of the Conservancy Boards, or by public opinion, to purchase lands at figures ranging from $300 to $1,500 per acre, upon which to utilize sewage in irrigation.

At Croydon, six years after irrigation with sewage began, land in the immediate vicinity of the farm where it was used had increased from £250 to £1,000 per acre. This fact shows two things—the immense price which has to be paid for land near the cities for irrigation, and hence the great drawback to the general introduction of this method of disposing of sewage; and the fact that the sewage farm could not have been an objectionable neighbor, otherwise the land would certainly not have increased so in value alongside of it. (Folsom, p. 341.)

It is no wonder, then, that there has been great opposition to the adoption of irrigation, for in fact in many instances, as is alleged, it is simply impossible to get land enough for the larger cities without pumping the sewage a number of miles, necessitating great expense for outfall and power works and annual charges for cost of operation.

Taking these facts into consideration, and the other circumstances that contribute towards making a sewage irrigation farm a troublesome and not profitable property for a municipal corporation to handle in England, it is no wonder that many devices and processes have come to public notice, the owners or advocates of which claiming for them the power to do away with all the embarrassments of the problems of sewage disposal. In fact such schemes may be numbered at least by hundreds.

FILTRATION.

Filtration was at first alleged to be the panacea for all evil caused by sewage waters ; and forthwith artificial filters of all conceivable patterns and compositions were designed and experimented with. There was "upward filtration," where the liquid was forced upward through filters, leaving its heavier suspended matters below, to be removed as "sludge;" and there was "lateral filtration," where the filter was upright, as a partition or wall, and the liquid thus passed through from one tank to another ; and, again, "downward filtration," where the liquid passed downward by gravity through the filter bed. And these filter beds were composed of every conceivable material and combination of materials, ranging from gravel, coarse and fine, through coarse and fine sand, earths of various kinds, bone dust, wood charcoal, animal charcoal, thin boards with very small perforations, and many others besides.

The first Rivers Pollution Commission tried some experiments upon the filtration of sewage through various soils, and they reported, in 1868, "that the process of filtration through gravel, sand, chalk, or certain kinds of soil, if properly carried out, is the most effective means of purifying sewage." (Rep. Riv. Pol. Com., 1868, p. 60.)

But this meant filtration through lands, and the fact is, as experience has proved also, that filtration cannot be "properly carried out" in an artificial filter, because it costs too much to make and maintain one large enough, so that the filter must be a natural one—a piece of land of such soil and subsoil composition as to be favorable, and either naturally or artificially well underdrained ; and the process thus carried out is of course but one step—that of having a plant growth on the land—removed from irrigation.

The advocates of artificial filter beds for the purification, or the clarification even, of sewage, have long ago abandoned their ground, and filtration now finds its place as a sort of concentration of irrigation.

The *Intermittent downward filtration*, heretofore spoken of, being the application of sewage to deeply drained land, in the proportion of ten to twelve times as great a quantity to the acre as in ordinary irrigation practice, at the sacrifice of crop growth and all but occasional cultivation of the soil, is of this character, and it is advocated chiefly as a substitute for irrigation when lands cannot be obtained in sufficient quantity for the latter, and as a supplement to irrigation for the purpose of disposing of the sewage when the crops do not need to be watered.

PRECIPITATION.

The well known properties of alum, lime, and alumina, whereby solid matters carried in suspension in water are made to settle to the bottom when the fluid is in a moderate state of rest, were long ago availed of to extract the noxious matters from sewage, and a number of processes based upon the use of these precipitants, singly and in combination, in various proportions with each other, and a host of still other substances, have been devised, patented, and tried—the most of them only to be discarded as worthless or too expensive in application.

Some, however, appear to have given a measure of satisfaction under conditions where suitable land could not be obtained for irrigation, so that, without intending to specify any as very much better than the others, it may be well to review those which I find most prominently mentioned as having been submitted to practical trial, although it is alleged by some authorities that these all have failed or are too expensive in application for general use, where it is desired to so far purify the sewage as to fit the effluent water for admission into any inland stream.

The *Coventry Process*, so called because of its adoption at the town of Coventry, in Warwickshire, employs salts of alumina as the chief precipitating agent.

At Coventry about 2,000,000 gallons per day of sewage, "extremely foul, and colored by refuse dye, etc., thrown into the sewers from numerous silk dyeing works, varnish works, etc." are treated by this process.

Four tanks built into the ground are used, the sewage constantly flowing through three of them, while the other is being cleaned. The sewage is first screened, to take out large floating solid matter, then treated to a dose of a solution of sulphate of alumina, prepared in a cheap way by treating shale with sulphuric acid; then it receives a charge of milk of lime, and, having dropped its solid matter in the tanks, the clarified water escaping from the tanks over weirs "in a fair state of purity," is then conveyed to filter beds, covering in all nine acres of land, where it is filtered, the beds being used alternately, and the water finally passes into the river Shurburne.

The *Native Guano*, or *A, B, C Process*, consists mainly in the use of alum, blood, and clay as precipitants, the exact receipt embodying also magnesia, chloride of sodium, animal and vegetable charcoal, and some other ingredients, and the manner of application being in tanks.

It has been tried at eight or ten large towns and cities, with varying success so far as economy and efficiency are concerned.

The *Phosphate Process* consists in the use of phosphate of alumina and lime as precipitants; the former being a good fertilizer, it increases the value of the resulting "sludge" for manure and facilitates its sale.

The phosphate of alumina is mixed with sulphuric acid to make it soluble, after which it is added to the sewage, together with a certain quantity of lime to aid the precipitation.

This process, also, has had its applications, and there are accounts of its success.

Then there are a large number of processes which are not so prominently mentioned, but which have had their applications, and still have their advocates, as follows :

Bird's Process employs "sulphated clay," so called, being a mixture of sulphuric acid with common clay.

Stothert's Process employs lime, sulphate of alumina, sulphate of zinc, and charcoal.

Hille's Process employs lime, tar, salts of magnesium, and the products arising from the calcination of lime.

Collins' Process employs lime, carbon (a waste product of

prussiate of potash manufacture), house ashes, soda, and per-chloride of iron.

Holden's Process employs sulphate of iron, lime, coal dust, and clay.

Fulda's Process employs, principally, lime and sulphate of soda.

Blythe's Process employs superphosphate of lime with magnesia and lime.

Whittread's Process employs a mixture of dicalcic and mono-calcic phosphates and a little milk of lime, the object being to recover in the manure the whole of the phosphoric acid.

Campbell's Process employs phosphate of lime in a soluble state which is applied to the sewage, and then precipitated by a further addition of lime.

Hanson's Process employs lime, black ash, and red hæmatite treated with sulphuric acid.

Goodall's Process employs lime, animal carbon, ashes, and an iron liquor called sesqui-persulphate of iron.

The *Lime Process* is about the oldest method of artificially treating sewage waters. At first lime alone was used, but now some other ingredients are sometimes added.

It has been tried in more places than any other process, and it may be said of it that whereas it fails to *purify* the sewage, it is a good clarifier and perhaps fits the waters to be purified by application to land about as well as any of the more complicated manipulations, but is complained of as not a good deodorizer during the operation, and as forming too much sludge of a low manurial value.

These are a few of a good many processes which may be found quite fully described in the reports of the Rivers Pollution Commission, in special papers brought before the Society of Arts, the Institution of Civil Engineers, and the Association of Sanitary Engineers, and briefly described or alluded to in the works of Corfield, Robinson, and Melliss, the report of Dr. Folsom, and elsewhere.

The record of their practical application at many different cities, towns, and burroughs under varying circumstances, the discussions of their merits which have occurred before the various societies mentioned, and the reports on their results made by various committees, commissions, etc., are, to say the least, decidedly confusing.

Taking them all together, I find it generally held by the authorities, and in fact most all who participate in the discussions, except those interested in the patent rights to the processes, or who want to adopt some such method of preparing sewage water for admission into a stream, to save a greater outlay for some other works, so far as I am able to judge, that they do *clarify* the liquid—precipitate the solid matter held in suspension; that some are decidedly more economical than others in the accomplishment of this result; that some, a few, perhaps, accomplish more than a mere clarification, and remove matters held in solution; that economy here also is variable; and that none of them so far *purify* the water as should render it admissible into a stream; but that it can readily be so purified by filtration through or use in irrigation on a small area of land after such clarification.

SOME AUTHORITIES.

Certain it is that the artificial treatment of sewage by either filtration, or chemical or mechanical precipitation, fails to purify the water and leaves it in a condition dangerous to be taken into the human system, even in a most diluted form.

First Rivers Pollution Commission.

The First Rivers Pollution Commission reported: "As "applied to sewage, disinfectants do not disinfect and filter "beds do not filter.* Both attempts have been costly failures."

---

* This applies to artificial filter beds and not to natural filtration through lands.

Sewage of Towns Commission.

The Sewage of Towns Commission reported that artificial filtration had been given up because "the filters choke imme-"diately and become impervious to the passage of the liquid."

Rivers Pollution Commission.

The Rivers Pollution Commission in 1858 and the Local Government Board in 1876 speak favorably of the deodorizing and clarify action of several precipitating processes, saying in substance that no nuisance in the way of odor arises from their proper application, nor does the effluent water offend the nostrils or eye, but they deny the efficiency of any such process in the way of the *purification* of the water.

Executive Committee of the Society of Arts Conference.

The Executive Committee of the Society of Arts Conference on Sewage, reported that by some of the precipitation processes, combined with filtration, "a sufficiently purified effluent can be "produced for discharge, without injurious results, into water-"courses and rivers, of sufficient magnitude for its considerable "dilution; and that for many towns, where land is not readily "obtainable at a moderate price, those particular processes "afford the most suitable means of disposing of water-carried "sewage."

This is the most favorable opinion I have found of these chemical processes, coming from a source other than individual, such as I have hitherto mentioned; and even this opinion is not to be ranked with those of the Government Commissioners appointed for that purpose, one of which is as follows:

Second Rivers Pollution Commission.

The Rivers Pollution Com'nission, of which Doctor Frankland was at the head as expert chemist, in their report of 1874 (the sixth), under the head of *"The possibility of rendering polluted water again wholesome"* (p. 427), say:

"Of all the processes which have been proposed for the purification "of sewage, or of water polluted by excrementitious matters, there is

8

"not one which is sufficiently effective to warrant the use, for dietetic "purposes, of water which has been so contaminated."

This opinion, of course, applies to artificial processes only. The conclusion of this Commission, with respect to the efficiency of irrigation as a process of purifying sewage, is elsewhere cited.

Dr. Folsom.

Dr. Folsom, who examined the subject personally for the Massachusetts Board of Health in 1875, reported as follows:

"In France and Germany the precipitating processes have been "given up as inefficient. In England a new successful patent process "is hawked about every few months, to be soon found only an addi- "tion to the list of failures; and the public is bewildered by the maze "of conflicting statements and propositions. In some cases, how- "ever, cities have been driven to the precipitating process because "they could not get sufficient land to deal with their sewage in any "other way." (Work cited, p. 333.)

This opinion is worthy of all credence, considering the source it comes from and the disinterested attitude occupied by the authority.

Bailey Denton.

In concluding this branch of the subject, I present extracts from the Lectures of Mr. Denton, to which I have before referred. They are selected and arranged so as to give an idea in a small space of the view this authority takes of the subject.

Until recently the laws of England required the liquid sew-age of towns to be conducted into rivers, etc.:

"Under the altered state of the laws towns must abstain from so "discharging until it has been freed '*from all* foul and noxious mat- "'ters' by the best practicable and reasonably available means." (Bailey Denton, Lectures, p. 248.)

In this respect towns are to be divided into three classes:

I. Seaboard towns.

II. Towns bordering tidal rivers or estuaries.

III. Towns adjacent to inland rivers and streams.

Discharging into the Sea.

" The possibility of discharging sewage into the sea unobjectionably
" only exists where the shore is not used for bathing or for recreation,
" and where the town does not extend down to the water's edge."

* * * * * * * * * * *

Thus it is often the case " that, even in seaboard towns, the sew-
" age, before it is discharged, should not only be clarified, but that
" everything should be done within reasonable limits to secure a con-
" stant outflow, independently of the tide."

* * * * * * * * * * *

" One or the other of the tried chemical precipitation processes
" will effect the required clarification of the sewage of this class of
" towns where land cannot be obtained." (Work cited, pp. 177–178.)

Discharging into Tidal Rivers and Estuaries.

"A considerable number of towns in this country are situated on
" the shores of tidal waters, some of which reach far inland. The
" difficulty of satisfactorily dealing with sewage which can only thus
" be carried to the sea by the ebb and flow of the tide is very con-
" siderable."

" The banks or shores of these waters generally consist of mud,
" and are exposed to the atmosphere for a sufficient time during each
" tide to give off in extremely hot weather an intolerable stench,
" which is necessarily made worse by mixture with sewage."

" In dealing with towns on tidal rivers it becomes the duty of the
" engineer to treat the liquid refuse differently from the way in which
" he would dispose of the sewage of either a town directly on the
" seaboard or situated on an inland river."

" The most rational view of the matter is, that while the sewage
" discharged from seaboard towns directly into the sea may be simply
" clarified, that which is discharged into tidal rivers, the waters of
" which are never used as sources of potable waters, should be
" cleansed of its putrescible matters up to a certain standard, which
" though less stringent than that applied to inland rivers, should be
" sufficiently high to prevent its causing the nuisance of which I have
" spoken." * * * * * * " These standards,
" it is declared, can be reached by several of the processes which I
" shall hereafter explain." (Work cited, p. 179.)

Discharging into Rivers far Inland.

" It is not only reasonable, but positively necessary, that considera-
" tions altogether different from those ruling in the case of seaboard
" towns should determine the mode of disposing of the sewage of
" inland towns.

" The effluent water in such cases should, indeed, be 'freed of all
" 'foul or noxious matter' (Public Health Act, 1875, clause 17),
" without compromise, and the law should be exercised without hesi-
" tation.

" The influence of the opposition of manufacturers upon the past
" and present governments has resulted in a temporary respite, and
" some ground has been lost by temporizing which had previously
" been gained by slow and certain steps; but when saying this it is
" impossible to evade the conclusion that the perfect and permanent
" cleansing of sewage will be sooner or later insisted upon by every
" voice in the country, and by no persons more decidedly than by
" the manufacturers themselves." (Work cited, pp. 180–182.)

Disposal of the Sewage of Villages and Hamlets.

" The remarks upon the disposal of liquid refuse of towns apply
" equally to villages. * * * * It has been taken for granted
" by most persons—simply because the point has not been thor-
" oughly discussed—that if solid refuse (kitchen and shop refuse,
" not sewage matter) is disposed of in some approved manner, very
" small places may turn their sewage water into the nearest water-
" course. This impression will have but a transient existence, though
" the money now being spent in temporizing with difficulties and in
" endeavoring to evade the law is very considerable. I feel bound
" to assert, though, * * * that there is no other way of satisfac-
" torily disposing of the liquid refuse of any community than by a
" common water-tight sewer, which shall collect and discharge it *for*
" *appropriate treatment.* This cannot be too well understood, for
" the precise mode of disposing of liquid sewage becomes compara-
" tively easy directly it is determined to collect and deliver it at a
" given point." (Work cited, pp. 182–183.)

As elsewhere noted, this authority favors *irrigation* where
land enough can be had; *intermittent downward filtration*,
through land prepared for the purpose, where sufficient land
for irrigation can not be had; and the *precipitating process*
where the land available is still more restricted, or not suitable
for the other mentioned methods of treatment.

CONCLUSION.

It is unnecessary to pursue this branch of the subject
further at present. The conclusions to be drawn are:

That if it is advisable to clarify—precipitate the solid matter held in suspension—the sewage at your institution, it can
be done, and with the detailed records of ample experience at
command to guide in the work; but that we can *not purify*
the waters as they should be purified, by any of these precipitation processes alone, unless we should be more successful
than the best authorities say such work has been in older
countries.

WHAT IS TO BE DONE WITH SEWAGE?

PART IV—THE DISPOSAL OF THE ASYLUM SEWAGE.

SHALL THE SEWAGE BE CARRIED AWAY?

And now for the application to the case in hand, of the facts and conclusions brought forward in the review of the Sewage-disposal question which I have presented in the preceding three chapters.

It has been proposed to conduct the asylum sewage (1) to the San Joaquin River, and dispose of it by mingling with the river waters ; or, failing in sufficient money to carry out this work, (2) to put it in Stockton Slough at some point west of the city limits ; or, as an alternative, (3) to extend the North Street canal to the river, and use it as an outfall for sewage at some point undefined; and I am called upon to say whether or not it is advisable for the Board of Directors to adopt either one of these outfalls and construct works in accordance therewith.

THE SANITARY ASPECT OF THE QUESTION.

The San Joaquin as an Outfall.

With respect to the first proposition—turning the sewage into the San Joaquin River—I am by no means satisfied that the deposit of the comparatively small amount of fouled liquid which your institution produces, into the river, would pollute its waters so as to be noticeable ; and were the question of no broader scope than one of policy or expediency on this footing, I would not be prepared, in the interest of undefiled river waters alone, to advise against the act.

But the question could not by any one be thus easily dismissed, for the deposit of this sewage in the river would be but the beginning of other acts of the same kind, and greater in degree, which quite likely would constitute a nuisance that soon would be cause for complaint by the casual observer even. In point of fact, the deposit of any such foul water in a running stream of this size, is held by the great bulk of scientific authority to materially pollute its waters, under ordinary circumstances, as I have already shown. So that even if the result of the deposit of the asylum sewage in the San Joaquin River was not *noticeably* objectionable, the justification of it on that ground would be a mere subterfuge, liable at any time to be laid bare, should any competent person take hold of the matter with the view of stopping such deposit.

If, as above, a private individual, or any organization, would not be justified in setting a bad example by thus disposing of sewage, and doing an act which, although not noticeably objectionable, could be exposed as a material and dangerous pollution of the waters of a public stream, still less would you, as officers of the State, be held blameless for such act.

The Stockton Slough as an Outfall.

As to the use of Stockton Slough, or any part of it, as an outfall for the asylum sewage, I am clearly of the opinion that such use would soon result in the pollution of its waters to such an extent that it would be noticeable to the eye of the casual observer for at least six months in the year; that in a very few years the bed of the slough in the neighborhood of the outfall, and above and below it, would become so charged with putrescible matter as to give off foul odors and deleterious gases, and that the solid matter of your sewage, amounting to 1,000 to 1,500 cubic feet, yearly, would settle in the slough channel, and not be carried away into the river.

It takes a water current velocity of two and a half to three and a quarter feet per second to hold in suspension—keep from settling—the suspended matters of sewage, and no such velocity now ever exists in Stockton Slough above the mouth of Mormon Slough, and below the mouth of Mormon Slough only for the few days of the highest floods.

The Stockton channel is a mere dead-end basin, without fixed water currents, for the greater portion of each year. A good part of this time—that portion when the river is high and the Mormon Slough is not in flood—there is not even a material tidal action in this basin. And when the water is low the tidal movement is only about two and a half feet.

Knowing the section of the channel at its mouth, the area and depth, and consequently the volume of the tidal prism above that point, and the time of tidal movement, as I do from surveys, with sufficient accuracy for this purpose, I find that the average velocity of tidal currents at the mouth must be even less than one foot a second, and that the maximum can rarely, if ever, exceed two feet, and that must be for a very short time at each tide.

This estimate is for the section at the mouth of the channel ; of course the rates diminish for each section above, until there is no perceptible current made by the tide much above Mormon Slough; the movement of the waters in the down-stream half of the channel alternately backing up and lowering those in the up-stream end.

Thus any disposal of sewage in this channel above the mouth of Mormon Slough would, so far as tidal current influence is concerned, be received in a pond almost without current, and disposal below that point would be in a channel with current insufficient to hold the solid matters in suspension, and that, too, running alternately up and down, so as to act both ways.

The water circulation in the upper half of Stockton Slough is kept up more by the influence of the wind than by tide. The trade winds of Summer blow almost directly up the channel, creating a surface current in that direction, which of course results in a sub-surface or bottom current in the opposite direction. Observation in other similar water basins shows these rules of circulation generally to prevail; and my own observation of Stockton channel leads me to believe that it presents no exception.

Sewage matter dumped into this channel would in part be swept up stream as well as down, and be simply spread along the bottom of the waterway.

It has been proposed to deposit the sewage at a point where some dead-end slough joins the main channel, making a back-water reservoir for the sewage, which would be emptied at low tide.

Under the circumstances and laws I have pointed out, a little reflection will show to any one, I hope, that this would be no safeguard against the evils of which I speak as results.

If there were tidal area enough towards the upper end of this slough in which to impound water at high tide by a dam, and let it out with a rush as the tide receded, some good might be thus effected, or, rather, harm prevented. But the circumstances are such as not to admit of any such arrangement at small cost, or any such cost, at least, as you would be justified in incurring for your purposes.

When sewage is put into tidal waters of this character, or even in a tidal river, the best way to insure its being moved to advantage, is to store it in a tank until the turn of the tide and then let it out, and also flush the channel, as I have indicated above, from a tidal reservoir.

The side channel dumpage would create a nuisance in less time than dumpage into the main slough, for the side channel itself would soon silt up and become a bed of festering matter to poison the air of the whole neighborhood.

The North Canal as an Outfall.

It has been proposed to continue the North Street canal through to the San Joaquin River; to use it as an outfall channel, or, to lay a pipe in it to be used as a main outfall sewer, or to lay a pipe for this purpose in the embankment bordering it.

This canal would for eight or nine thousand feet of its

length be located through the tule swamp whose surface is three to five feet below the level of ordinary high water in the river; and, being joined to the river, it would have to be flanked by embankments on each side, varying in height from six to eight feet, to preserve it as a canal.

During the greater portion of each year the canal would be simply a dead-end tidal channel, that would not keep itself clear of silt from natural washings, much less carry away the solid matter of sewage should it be deposited therein. This canal would require a constant flow of seventy-five to one hundred cubic feet of water per second to make it self-cleansing, and where any such supply can be had to feed it, for at least eight months in each year, I am at a loss to know.

The city of Sacramento has just such a canal for an outfall channel for its sewage waters. Under a city ordinance every house drain has to connect with a cesspool, so that the solid matter settles therein, and the overflow liquid, only, reaches the sewers and through them the canal. Yet this canal, receiving but little solid matter, and with greater grade than can be had in 10,000 feet of the proposed extension of the North Street canal of Stockton, and receiving a larger amount of sewage than that would receive (giving it a better flow on the average, of course), is an object that, I am satisfied, the owners of property in Stockton would not like to have transferred to their neighborhood, and which the Sacramentans would quickly get rid of, if they could at any outlay of money which the city could immediately afford.

If the proposed North Street canal were not carried through to the river, the sewage would spread over private lands.

If the pipe were laid in the canal through which to run sewage, as has been proposed, it would be below water and impossible to get at for repairs, would be broken by unequal settlement in the soft ground, and have to be flushed out under considerable pressure, artificially applied, during at least six months of the year when the river was not nearly at its lowest stage.

9

If a sewer pipe were laid in the embankment, it would be broken by unequal settlement of the bank, unless that bank were specially built to sustain it, at very considerable extra expense, and there are other objections to this arrangement which I mention in the last part of this report.

If a sewer pipe is to be laid from the asylum, or the northern part of the city of Stockton, to the San Joaquin River, unless a very considerable amount of money is to be expended in constructing this canal and building and protecting its banks, it (the pipe) should be laid down along the northern bank of the Stockton channel, where the ground is most firm, where it will be most accessible, cheap of construction, and economical in maintenance. It should be put upon a good artificial foundation wherever the natural ground is not sufficiently firm, and be so located as to be within (north of) the line of levee that doubtless some day will be erected there.

In short, I do not see that the asylum sewage problem, up to this point of our consideration of it, has, properly, anything to do with the North Street canal or its extension.

The agricultural drainage from the asylum grounds, inclusive of the ground filtered by sewage waters, should the sewage be used properly in the irrigation of those grounds, might well find an outfall by that canal; but the *sewage* should not go into it, nor should it go along it or its embankment, in a pipe, unless, as I have said, there is to be an embankment specially built for the purpose of holding such pipe, and unless works are to be here carried out, in connection therewith, very much more expensive and elaborate than you would be justified in undertaking, except as a small part of the city of Stockton.

I now respectfully call your attention to another aspect of this question of outfall into the San Joaquin River or any of its arms.

The Legal Aspect of the Question.

The State, the Guardian of the Streams.

The State is the guardian of the public streams, particularly of those which are navigable. If anything is done which pollutes the waters of such streams, the authority of the State would or should be exercised to stop it. Perhaps this practice of dumping sewage into streams will be resorted to in this State by town authorities as a convenient, and, apparently to them, cheap way of getting rid of it. Perhaps the subject will be tampered with and temporized with here, just as it has been elsewhere, until some flagrant nuisances have been created—until the beds of our watercourses have been poisoned—when the State will be called upon to stop the practice.

But when this time comes it should not be of record that the State herself, by the act of the Directors of the Stockton Insane Asylum, set the bad example which, followed out, will have led to the pollution of her streams, the waste of money in town sewerage works that will have to be remodelled, and probably will have conduced to the propagation of some of those disease scourges the names of which, even, fill many people with dread.

Or, perhaps, I may be wrong when I say that this evil practice of fouling river waters with sewage will probably grow up here ; I hope so, but at any rate it will be well to set the example of a right and proper mode of disposing of sewage; and while there might be blame in future store for State authorities who set a bad example, there may be praise awaiting the carrying out of a good example, and material benefit to the citizens of the State by thus showing town authorities what should be done and how to do it in this respect.

At any rate, unpopular though it may be, and "ahead of the times" here, or savoring of refinement of policy not justified by the facts, as it may seem to the many persons who have not really studied the matter, and who will naturally tend to the easiest solution, for the time being, of this sewage disposal problem here, as many other good people have done elsewhere, it is clearly my duty to point out the danger ahead and advise against taking the channel which experience has so fully shown to be filled with rocks and shoals and wrecks, further on.

I see no reason why we, though far from the scenes of mature experience on this sewage question, should fall into the same errors (and there are hundreds of them besides the one I have pointed out) that the local authorities of England and Germany and France have waded through, or are still floundering in, at such enormous expense to their "rate payers." For we have only to look thoroughly into the subject—to go below the scum of books written merely for popular sale—and devote some systematic study to the detailed professional accounts of what others have done, rather than to trust to the inspiration of "local talent," and be led by shallow efforts at economizing at the inauguration of sewerage systems.

California Penal Code.

Beyond the matter of policy in this question of sewage disposal for your institution, lies the facts of the law.

Section 374 of the Penal Code of the State, as amended in 1875-76, reads as follows :

" Every person who puts the carcass of any dead animal, or the
" offal from any slaughter-pen, corral, or butcher shop, into any river,
" creek, pond, reservoir, stream, street, alley, public highway, or road
" in common use, or who attempts to destroy the same by fire within
" one fourth of a mile of any city, town, or village, and every person
" who puts the carcass of any dead animal, or any offal of any kind,
" in or upon the borders of any stream, pond, lake, or reservoir,
" from which water is drawn for the supply of the inhabitants of any
" city, city and county, or any town, in this State, so that the drain-
" age from such carcass or offal may be taken up by or in such
" stream, pond, lake, or reservoir, or who allows the carcass of any
" dead animal, or any offal of any kind, to remain in or upon the
" borders of any such stream, pond, lake, or reservoir, within the ·
" boundaries of any lands owned or occupied by him, or who keeps
" any horses, mules, cattle, swine, sheep, or live stock of any kind,
" penned, corraled, or housed on, over, or on the borders of any
" such stream, pond, lake, or reservoir, so that the waters thereof
" shall become polluted by reason thereof, is guilty of a misdemeanor,
" and upon conviction thereof shall be punished as prescribed in
" Section 377 of this Code. (In effect March 23, 1876.)

This law does not say " sewage" or "sewage matter;" but it certainly seems to me that it specifies infinitely *less offensive acts* than that of depositing several cubic feet daily of the most foul and dangerous offal known, in a stream, and says that the person found doing either of them shall be deemed guilty of a misdemeanor, and punished accordingly.

The solid matter of the asylum sewage, to say nothing of the liquid, which is very much greater in bulk, would about equal a good sized calf, at the verge of decomposition, daily, deposit it where you will.

The Law of Nuisances.

Without in any way attempting to assume the part of your legal adviser, but rather to bring to your attention some primary points of the law, in order that you may see the necessity for taking advice of your proper legal counselor before making a step which may lead to trouble, should you be inclined to put the sewage of your institution into any stream or ditch, I recommend to your reading the thirteenth chapter of "Wood on Nuisances," edition of 1883, a work which I believe stands high as a legal text-book.

You will there find that "the right of a riparian owner to " have the water of a stream come to him in its natural purity " is as well recognized as the right to have it flow to his land;" that "the Legislature," even, "has not the power to authorize " the use " of a navigable stream "in such a way as to destroy " its use by riparian owners " for drinking or "primary pur- " poses," "without compensation ; that the fact of its being a " public convenience to dispose of offal in a river, is no excuse " in the eyes of the law ;" that "neither does it make any " difference or in any measure operate as an excuse that the " nuisance cannot be obviated without great expense, or that " the plaintiff himself could obviate the injury at a trifling " expense ;" that the question of distance which the offensive matter may be transported does not operate as an excuse ; that, in the words of a leading English decision, " the pollution " of the waters of a navigable stream so as to destroy their " value for *primary* purposes, by leading into the same the " sewage of the town, is a nuisance," and "the fact that sewage " has been sent there for many years does not give a prescrip- " tive right to continue it, when, *by the increase therein*, it " becomes a nuisance."

These, and many more sentences in the same vein, seem to

be right to the point, and worthy of attention ; for, the exceptions to the rule given by the same authority, are, (1) when the pollution is slight and not appreciable, or (2) when the increase of pollution is not noticeable.

The test of pollution must ever be a scientific one, for water may be absolutely poisonous from animal organisms, and still be sweet to the taste, without odor, sparkling, and attractive to the eye; and chemistry tells us that *any* pollution of water with sewage *is material*, dangerous, and should not be permitted even when the water is only occasionally used for drinking purposes, or by a few persons only.

The Civil Code of California.

Our Civil Code (Sec. 3479) says that anything which " *offends decency*" is a nuisance, or that "unlawfully interferes with, obstructs, or tends to obstruct, or renders dangerous for passage, any lake, or navigable river, bay, stream, canal, or basin," etc.

You soon will have two thousand people at your institution. The combined personal offal of this number of human beings, men, women, and children averaged, is one hundred and forty-four thousand pounds of solid matter, and one million nine hundred thousand pounds of liquid, per year.

It may be well to ask whether it would "offend decency" to put this matter into the Stockton Slough, the North Street canal, or even the San Joaquin River; and it may be well to ask whether it would "tend to obstruct" the passage of boats, etc., to put this matter into the slough or river.

Of course, I cannot advise you on these points, but simply bring them to your notice that you may inquire further from the right source for legal advice.

CAN THE SEWAGE BE RETAINED ON THE ASYLUM GROUNDS?

As the alternative to the removal of the sewage from your institution to the river or other tide-water outfall, the question presented is: can the sewage be retained upon the asylum grounds without producing effects detrimental to the sanitary condition of the neighborhood—the health and comfort of persons there resident?

To this question I reply YES, in my judgment this can be done, and, more too, the sewage is valuable and should not be wasted.

But, it will be answered: this sewage matter has been thus utilized for years in the past, until now it has become a nuisance, and its removal is demanded alike for the good of the health and comfort of the residents roundabout.

That there are offensive odors pervading these grounds during the warm and still Summer and Fall months, that the sewage itself at such times is quite offensive, that the effect in the neighborhood of the cesspool where it is collected is very repulsive, and that this state of things is not only disagreeable but alarming and demands speedy correction, I am prompt to admit; but that the mentioned effects are due to sewage irrigation, I do not admit.

The Present Arrangements.

With several thousand feet of large wooden box drain, which must by this time be filled with decomposing and most foul matter, leading from the buildings through the grounds to the cesspool; with a great pit or hole in the ground, unlined, uncovered, which has for years been the receptacle for all this matter, for a cesspool, the earth of its sides and bottom soaked and reeking with corrupted matter; with an open bucket pump to raise the filthy liquid, all exposed to the sun and air, dripping and dirty the year around; with open wooden flumes, soaked with the fermenting matter of months ago, laid about the grounds for the distribution of the sewage in irrigation; with these arrangements, I say, you have quite sufficient cause for emanations of the most repulsive kind and far-reaching power, without attributing any part of such noticed effects to the sewage irrigated grounds themselves.

If these grounds contribute in any material degree to this nuisance, it is for reasons of insufficient preparation of them

for irrigation, and unsuitable arrangements for the distribution
of the waters in irrigation, to wit :

1. Because they are not underdrained, and consequently
(a) do not take the sewage water promptly as they should,
(b) at times become over-saturated and give off their superfluous moisture by evaporation from the surface instead of by
underdrainage as they should, (c) do not become promptly
aerified after each irrigation, and (d) swell upon being soaked
and crack open on becoming dry.

2. Because in distribution, the sewage is run long distances
in shallow open ditches, thus permitting the soil inclosing
these channel-ways to become overcharged with the liquid
and the bottom and sides of the ditches to become coated
with sewage sediment, so that when the irrigation is stopped
and water withdrawn from any such ditch there is a film or
deposit of matter left in it—not taken into the soil and
deodorized as it should be by it. And finally,

3. Because the irrigation is not carried on with dispatch
and promptness, but the waters are left running for hours,
slowly finding their way about the grounds. This is more the
outcome of inefficient distributing works, perhaps, than of
poor management in their use.

Proper Arrangements to be Made.

In my judgment, when the foul wooden box-drains shall
have been removed, and the ditches in which they have lain
have been refilled with fresh soil mixed with lime, when the
earthen pit cesspool shall have been thoroughly emptied,
cleansed, and in like manner filled up; when the wooden box
distributing troughs or flumes and open bucket pumps shall
have been put well out of the way; when the sewage is conducted from the buildings in good ironstone glazed sewer
pipes laid with neat cement joints, into a covered vat or tank
with concrete floor and walls neatly rendered in cement, and
is then pumped by some suitable closed pump through proper
pipes and thus distributed about the grounds so that it will

never have to run more than a hundred feet through an open ditch; when these grounds are underdrained and about twenty acres of them specially prepared for sewage irrigation, and twenty acres more kept in such condition of cultivation that the sewage can occasionally be put thereon to advantage, then—when these things are done—your sewage waters can be kept at home without nuisance or offense to any one and with great advantage to the economy of your institution.

If anything further is required to insure perfect sanitary results, I should first look to your house plumbing and indoor drainage work. All the outside work may be perfect, but with these defective, as they are in ninety-nine cases out of every hundred in this State, and, as I have no doubt they are in the older buildings at least of your institution, no amount of conducting the sewage away or properly using it on the grounds will accomplish the result which should be your primary object to attain.

If after these works are tried, it appears desirable to make assurance doubly sure in the line of complete sanitary treatment of your sewage, which I do not think will be the case, it will then be time to erect a proper tank or tanks, and by the use of some one of the processes for precipitation heretofore described, clarify your sewage before applying the water to the land, and promptly mixing the precipitated matter with ashes, dry stable manure, and dry earth, sell it for manure, or apply it at the proper season to enrich the fields and gardens of your reservation.

I am satisfied for the present, however, that with proper means of collecting and promptly and rapidly distributing your sewage on well prepared grounds, and with a skillful use of these appliances, you will not need any precipitating tanks, for you have ample grounds to spare upon which, if properly prepared and arranged, to put the sewage of 6,000 people, at almost the minimum rate at which such disposal is made in older countries, in instances where no nuisances or bad effect of any kind is produced.

Your land, soil and subsoil, to be sure, is not of the most favorable quality for irrigation. It is a heavy adobe soil, varying in depth from two to four feet, on a clay marl subsoil; whereas it should to best advantage be of lighter, more sandy, texture, deeper and on a more open subsoil. But thorough tile underdrainage will do much to correct the defects of the soil and make up for the want of a porous subsoil and the absence of natural drainage-ways in the vicinity.

This absence of natural drainage-ways, and the small slope of the plain, rendering it difficult to get a good gravity outfall for the under-drainage of the land, it may be necessary and probably will, at times during the rainy season at least, to lead the drainage waters into a well, and pump them out into some neighboring natural surface drainage channel, or into the North Street canal. These waters, of course, will be inoffensive and nearly if not quite as pure as any drainage waters, for they will be in part rain waters, and will all have passed through the soil, and have been subjected, as we have seen, to the best known process for their purification—the natural one of land filtration and plant action—and hence they can be discharged anywhere that any waters may be run, without giving cause for complaint. Such drainage waters are freely admitted into all streams in the countries where this subject has received so much attention, and where the war against sewage pollutions is most earnestly carried on.

Beyond these arrangements, there should be some systematic crop rotation established for your grounds, whereunder your sewage can be utilized in the watering of such plants as best receive it and thrive by its use, while other crops which we know do not do well under its influence should be irrigated with pure water.

Sewage-Farming and Drainage.

An essential feature of preparation, natural or artificial, for successful irrigation—good crop returns and good sanitary condition of the fields and neighborhood—when carried on with the purest waters even, is perfect drainage and a well aerated soil. Where these are absent, crops will after awhile begin to fail, special plant diseases appear, malarial affections will become prevalent amongst the people, and irrigation will be voted a failure and fraught with more harm than good.

There are localities where such conditions prevail, and such results are being encountered now in California. It is an old story in older countries, but here the question is not understood. All over this State where irrigation is practiced, provision for drainage will after awhile have to be made.

You cannot have a fine stand of alfalfa under irrigation on thirty to forty acres of your land, the soil and subsoil being as it is, and long preserve a good sanitary condition of your grounds and neighborhood, unless you drain them. If irrigation is to go on and be extended around your buildings, of the character that has been carried forward, there should be underdrainage, whether you use sewage waters or clear artesian well waters.

A sewage farm is what we choose to make it—unobjectionable as a neighbor if we will, very objectionable if we allow it to be.

Sewage waters are not offensive during the first twenty-four hours after their pollution, if they are kept from the sun, or in any event for the first eighteen to twenty hours, if retained in proper receptacles.

An essential feature of an unobjectionable sewage farm is an undefiled receptacle for the fresh sewage, which can be washed out and kept pure, and like means of distributing the sewage rapidly and to points near where it is to be absorbed by the ground. .

You have not any of these essentials to success in conducting your sewage irrigation. Let us provide them, and then see if anything more be needed.

CONCLUSION.

In carrying out these suggestions—by keeping your sewage at home and utilizing it on your grounds—you will be only doing what hundreds of other authorities in charge of similar institutions less favorably situated, with respect to climate at least, are doing or preparing to do, what hundreds of small and large towns are doing or preparing to do, what many others would do if the local circumstances would admit of it, and what is gradually being recognized throughout the world as the proper and only reasonable thing to be done with sewage.

Sanitary and engineering literature of this day and for the past ten years is replete with evidence of this fact, and with practical information as to how to insure success in such works. Your minds once made up to this course, and your work well done, you will have taken the right steps to accomplish your purpose of proper sanitation of your institution, and will have done nothing not necessary in any event.

The engineering aspect of your problem, with plans and estimates for your work, will be briefly set forth in the next and final part of this report.

www.ingramcontent.com/pod-product-compliance
Lightning Source LLC
Chambersburg PA
CBHW021526270326
41930CB00008B/1111

* 9 7 8 3 3 3 7 3 6 7 4 5 9 *